GITA
for the Young & the Urban

ALSO BY THE SAME AUTHOR

Shiva

Ask the Monk

Icons of Grace

ADVANCE PRAISE FOR THE BOOK

'In a world of burnout, anxiety and endless scrolling, here is a breath of spiritual clarity. In *Gita for the Young & the Urban*, Nityanand Charan Das brings the timeless voice of the Bhagavad Gita to today's youth, offering not just words but a way to live. This book is a friend for the restless soul.

'With warmth and simplicity, the Gita's wisdom is distilled into everyday insights—for anyone seeking peace and a deeper meaning to life'—**Shivika Goenka, founder, RP Goenka International School and The Gift Studio**

'Simple, digestible nuggets of wisdom, perfect for the young and urban but relatable to anyone with questions about the world around us'—**Divia Thani, writer and editor**

'Prabhuji presents the timeless wisdom of the Gita in a clear, accessible way, highlighting its core principles for everyday living. With simplicity and depth, he helps spiritual seekers understand and apply these teachings in practical, meaningful ways. A truly illuminating guide for daily spiritual practice'—**Arushi Agrawal, founder, Seva Home**

'Prabhuji's book beautifully distils the wisdom of the Bhagavad Gita into simple, engaging lessons for today's youth. It makes deep spiritual concepts accessible and relatable, inspiring young minds to reflect and grow'—**Sonakshi Agarwal, managing director, Sterlite EdIndia Foundation**

'The Gita explained not for sages in caves but for young minds in coffee shops and corporate cubicles. Spiritually rich. Culturally aware. Emotionally honest'—**Sakshi Chopra, managing director, Peak XV Partners**

GITA
for the Young & the Urban

UNPLUG FROM THE NOISE, TUNE INTO YOUR SOUL

Nityanand Charan Das

PENGUIN
ANANDA
An imprint of Penguin Random House

PENGUIN ANANDA

Penguin Ananda is an imprint of the Penguin Random House group of companies whose addresses can be found at global.penguinrandomhouse.com

Published by Penguin Random House India Pvt. Ltd
4th Floor, Capital Tower 1, MG Road,
Gurugram 122 002, Haryana, India

Penguin Random House India

First published in Penguin Ananda by Penguin Random House India 2025

10 9 8 7 6 5 4 3

ISBN 9780143469636

Typeset in Sabon LT Std by Manipal Technologies Limited, Manipal
Printed at Thomson Press India Ltd, New Delhi

www.penguin.co.in

To Srila Prabhupada
(founder-acharya of ISKCON),
who made the Bhagavad Gita a global name

Contents

Foreword

The Bhagavad Gita is one of the most profound spiritual texts ever written. For over 5000 years, it has served as a guiding light for seekers, philosophers, leaders and everyday individuals searching for purpose and clarity in life. It is not merely a book but a conversation—one that transcends time, culture and geography. In its 700 verses, the Gita encapsulates the deepest wisdom on human nature, duty, relationships, success, failure, happiness and self-realization. Yet despite its timeless relevance, many today—especially millennials and younger generations—struggle to connect with its teachings.

In an age of constant distraction, rapid technological advancement and ever-changing social dynamics, the pursuit of inner peace and fulfilment often takes a back seat. Today's youth are ambitious, driven and eager to make an impact, yet they frequently find themselves grappling with anxiety, self-doubt and existential questions. Amid the noise of social media, career pressures and personal challenges, the question arises: How can ancient wisdom be applied to modern life?

This is where *Gita for the Young and the Urban* by Nityanand Charan Das becomes crucial. With great insight and compassion, he distils the essential teachings of the Gita into a relatable, practical and engaging format for today's world. Rather than presenting it as a distant, esoteric scripture, he brings it alive as a manual for real-life situations—a road map for self-discovery, resilience and success.

Why Millennials Need the Gita More Than Ever

The millennial generation and Gen Z are often seen as restless, ambitious and deeply connected to technology. They seek instant gratification, constant validation and a fast-paced lifestyle. However, beneath this surface lies an inner turmoil—a quest for deeper meaning. The Gita offers precisely that: a blueprint for navigating life's complexities with wisdom and clarity.

One of the most powerful aspects of the Bhagavad Gita is its setting—on a battlefield. Arjuna, a warrior paralysed by doubt and fear, stands at a crossroads. He is overwhelmed by confusion, anxiety and moral dilemmas, much like the youth of today when faced with career choices, relationship struggles or ethical decisions. Krishna, his charioteer and spiritual guide, does not offer mere motivational words; instead, he imparts timeless wisdom that helps Arjuna shift his mindset, understand his dharma (duty) and act with conviction.

This is precisely what young people need today: not just encouragement but clarity. Not just motivation but direction. And not just success but fulfilment. The Gita teaches that true success is not merely about external achievements but about internal stability. It emphasizes that life is not about running away from challenges but about facing them with wisdom and detachment.

The Key Teachings of the Gita for the Youth

Throughout this book, Nityanand Charan Das masterfully highlights the key principles of the Bhagavad Gita that are most relevant to today's generation. A few of these include:

1. **The Art of Decision-Making:** The modern world bombards us with countless choices, leading to confusion and anxiety. The Gita teaches us how to make decisions based on wisdom rather than fleeting emotions.
2. **Overcoming Fear and Self-Doubt:** Fear of failure, rejection and uncertainty is common among young people. Krishna's words help cultivate courage, resilience and faith in the process of life.

3. **Detachment in a Hyperconnected World:** In an era of social media, comparisons and external validation, the Gita's lessons on detachment remind us to seek fulfilment from within rather than through likes, comments or approval.
4. **The Science of Work and Success:** Many believe that happiness lies in achieving results, but the Gita offers a different perspective. It teaches Karma Yoga—working with devotion and sincerity without attachment to the outcome.
5. **Inner Peace Amidst Chaos:** With mental health challenges on the rise, the Gita provides profound insights into controlling the mind, managing stress and attaining inner peace through spiritual discipline.

Making the Gita Relevant for Today

One of the biggest challenges in presenting the Bhagavad Gita to modern readers is bridging the gap between ancient wisdom and contemporary issues. Nityanand Charan Das achieves this beautifully by using real-life examples, relatable stories and practical applications of the Gita's teachings.

What sets this book apart is its conversational tone and its ability to engage younger audiences. Rather than being overly philosophical or academic, it speaks directly to the reader in a way that feels personal, insightful and immediately useful. It acknowledges the struggles of modern life while offering timeless solutions.

A Call to Action for Today's Youth

The Bhagavad Gita is not meant to be just read—it is meant to be lived. Its teachings are not confined to temples or spiritual discussions; they are meant for boardrooms, classrooms, relationships and everyday decisions. This book is an invitation for young people not merely to understand the Gita intellectually but to apply it in their lives.

In a world that often feels overwhelming, where external success can sometimes lead to internal emptiness, the Gita provides an anchor. It teaches that true fulfilment comes not from what we achieve but from how we live—with purpose, integrity and devotion.

As you embark on this journey through the pages of *Gita for the Young and the Urban*, I encourage you to read with an open heart and an open mind. This is not just another book; it is a conversation—one between Krishna and Arjuna, and now between you and your own inner self.

May this book serve as a guiding light, helping you navigate life's challenges with wisdom, strength and clarity. May it inspire you to rise above self-doubt, embrace your duty with courage and find true fulfilment in a world that is constantly changing.

And, most importantly, may it help you remember that no matter what happens in life, you are never alone—because Krishna's wisdom, like the Gita itself, will always be with you.

Gauranga Das,
monk, spiritual leader, author

Introduction

Why we should read the Bhagavad Gita—especially now.

In a world full of chaos, choices and constant scrolling, it's easy for us to feel lost. We're expected to succeed, smile, stay strong—and somehow figure out life, relationships, career, purpose and peace all at once. But where's the manual for all this?

There is one. It's called the Bhagavad Gita.

It's not a dusty old scripture meant only for priests or philosophers. It's a divine conversation between a warrior who's overwhelmed with anxiety (sounds familiar?) and his best friend, who just happens to be God.

Arjuna was stuck—emotionally, mentally, spiritually. He was questioning everything: What's the point of this struggle? Are we doing the right thing? Why does life feel so heavy? How do we find clarity?

That's when Krishna speaks.

And what He says isn't just for Arjuna—it's for us. Right here. Right now.

The Gita doesn't demand blind belief. It invites us to think deeply. It doesn't just preach—it empowers. It shows us how to live with courage in confusion, peace in pressure and purpose in a world that often seems purposeless.

Still wondering if it's relevant today? Let's ask ourselves:

- Have we ever struggled with overthinking?
- Ever felt unsure about our next step?
- Been let down by people or by our own expectations?
- Wanted to know who we really are, beyond our resumes, reels and relationships?

Then the Gita is our book.

It's not a book of 'don'ts'. It's a guide to real freedom—from fear, from failure, from the noise outside and the war within. It's Krishna speaking directly to our hearts. And we're not alone in turning to it. The Bhagavad Gita has been translated into over eighty languages and has sold millions of copies worldwide.

It's studied in Ivy League universities and quoted by thinkers, scientists, CEOs, athletes and monks alike. Even Albert Einstein and Steve Jobs found deep wisdom in its verses.

Initially, I thought of writing a verse-by-verse commentary on the Gita. But let's be honest—most of us, despite good intentions, struggle to go beyond a few chapters. Time is limited. Focus is harder than ever. And the Gita's wisdom is deep, layered and spread across eighteen chapters covering many profound themes.

So instead of a traditional commentary, I chose a different approach: We extracted the core themes, connected the dots across chapters and presented each major idea as its own exclusive chapter—clear, engaging and relatable.

The goal? To make the timeless message of the Gita accessible, powerful and life-changing—without feeling overwhelming.

And here's the best part: even if we read just one chapter with sincerity, it can begin to shift how we see life—and how we live it.

So, let's open it. We're not just opening a book. We're opening a conversation with God. And trust me—it will be the most meaningful conversation of our lives.

1

The Echo of Our Actions

Karma never forgets. No matter how powerful we are, no matter how much we possess—our past actions never leave us. They are like shadows, inseparably tied to us, silently shaping our destiny. The law of karma spares no one. The pain we inflict on others finds its way back to us, shattering our peace. This is why even the wealthiest, most successful people can be haunted by anxiety despite having everything that anyone in this world could aspire for. True power is not in possession, but in purity. True peace is not in luxury, but in righteousness.

The Bhagavad Gita opens with a single question from Dhritarashtra, a question that reveals the deep-seated fear lurking in his heart.

dhṛtarāṣṭra uvāca
dharma-kṣetre kuru-kṣetre

samavetā yuyutsavaḥ
māmakāḥ pāṇḍavāś caiva
kim akurvata sañjaya

Bhagavad Gita (1.1)

'O Sanjaya, after my sons and the sons of Pandu assembled in the place of pilgrimage at Kurukshetra, desiring to fight, what did they do?'

This question, on the surface, seems ordinary but in reality reveals the deep-seated fear consuming his heart. He is not an ordinary man—he is a king, the ruler of an empire. He commands a vast army, boasts of the support of invincible warriors like Bhishma and Drona and sits upon the throne of Hastinapura. Yet, despite all of this, he is restless. His mind is clouded with anxiety, his heart heavy with dread.

When Silence Becomes Sin

The law of karma is merciless—it does not discriminate between a king and a beggar, between the mighty and the weak. It is an eternal force, ensuring that the consequences of our actions return to us, whether we are prepared for them or not. Dhritarashtra, though blind in sight, was never blind to the injustice that his sons, led by Duryodhana, inflicted upon the Pandavas. He knew of their deceit, their cruelty, their numerous attempts to destroy their noble cousins. Yet, he chose silence. He chose inaction. And by doing so, he became as guilty as the wrongdoers themselves.

Now, Dhritarashtra is extremely fearful about the aftermath of the war, and he anticipates the worst possible outcome for his sons, who stand on the battlefield facing the mighty Pandavas. He is well aware of the strength of the Pandavas, but his fears are magnified by the knowledge that the place chosen for the war is the holy land of the Kurukshetra.

Why a Holy Place Feels Like a Curse

A holy place adds to the powers of holy people and takes away from the powers of unholy people. He knows that his sons, headed by Duryodhana, are unholy at heart and hence, fears for their lives.

In addition, Krishna is on the Pandavas' side as Arjuna's charioteer, always willing to guide them. Thus, the powers of the already mighty Pandavas have received a major boost. The king is also worried that due to the positive influence of the Kurukshetra, Duryodhana might have a change of heart and return the kingdom to the Pandavas without a fight. Dhritarashtra does not want any such compromise. He would like to hold on to the throne till his last breath. His concerns multiplying with the minute, he asks his secretary about the events on the battlefield.

However, if we analyse carefully, we realize that he hardly has any reason to worry. His sons' army is much bigger than that of the Pandavas. Duryodhana enjoys the support of invincible warriors like Bhishma and Drona and the finances and other logistics are on his side since he rules the kingdom.

What Goes Around, Comes Around

Then why is Dhritarashtra still fearful? It is because he is sinful. As per the law of karma, three people must share the fruits of karma equally: the doer, the director and the supporter. Dhritarashtra has been a constant supporter of his sons' conspiracies to harm and even kill the Pandavas. Thus, he shares the sin equally with his sons.

Sin is always accompanied by fear.

When we wrong or hurt someone, that person may not retaliate, either as a voluntary choice or due to them not being strong enough to do anything. It may prompt us to think: *What can he or she do to me?* But the pain that we have caused to a person, will certainly return to us from a different source in some way or the other, such that despite having everything, we will not be able to live in peace.

Creating mental distress, fear or anxiety in the mind is one of the ways in which the law of karma punishes wrongdoers. Thus, Dhritarashtra, despite apparently having everything in his support, is not peaceful. This is why even the wealthiest, most successful individuals—those who seemingly have everything—often battle inner demons of anxiety, guilt and restlessness. Outwardly, they may bask in luxury, but within, they are prisoners of their own conscience. They have comforts but no real happiness and peace because in the pursuit of success, or due to the ego brought on by this success, they have wronged others.

On the other hand, when we do good to others, they may not be in a position to, or choose to not, do good to us, but the rewards of the good work that we have done will certainly return to us in some way or other from a different source. Thus, we must keep up the good work and take extra care to not cause any deliberate inconvenience to anyone.

A life built on deception and wrongdoing may rise high, but it will never stand firm. But a life rooted in truth, in goodness, in selfless action—that is a life unshaken, a life of real strength and above all, a life of peace.

2

Guru

The Real Guide

Lost Without a Compass? Get a Guru

Have you ever felt like we were doing everything right, but life still didn't make sense?

We try to reason our way through problems. We consult friends, follow motivational videos, read self-help blogs and still—nothing seems clear. Our minds become a battlefield of doubt and emotion. We know something has to change, but we don't know what.

That's exactly where Arjuna found himself—right in the middle of the world's most decisive war, paralysed not by the enemy in front of him, but by the confusion within.

And then he did something extraordinary.

He stopped pretending he had all the answers. He put down his arguments. He bowed his head. And he said the words that changed everything:

kārpaṇya-doṣopahata-svabhāvaḥ
pṛcchāmi tvāṁ dharma-sammūḍha-cetāḥ
yac chreyaḥ syān niścitaṁ brūhi tan me
śiṣyas te 'haṁ śādhi māṁ tvāṁ prapannam

'Now I am confused about my duty and have lost all composure because of miserly weakness. In this condition I am asking You to tell me for certain what is best for me. Now I am Your disciple, and a soul surrendered unto You. Please instruct me.'

That moment wasn't just Arjuna's turning point—it's meant to be ours. This is the sacred moment when the seeker becomes a student. And Krishna becomes the Guru.

Let's explore why *this* surrender—choosing a spiritual guide—is not a sign of weakness but the beginning of true wisdom.

Higher Questions Need Higher Guidance

Human life is special. It is not simply meant to be wasted in materialistic pursuits centred around eating, sleeping, mating and defending, the four activities common between humans and animals. What separates humans from other species is that we are blessed with a superior intelligence and can thus seek answers to questions like: Who am I? Where do I come from and where will I go? What is the real goal of life? Who is God and what is my relationship with Him? How may I revive that relationship? How can I put an end to all my suffering?

If a human being is not aspiring for these higher goals, he is no better than an animal. The opportunity to enjoy our senses can be had in any species. A bird wakes up in the morning and questions, 'Where is my food? Where is my mother? Where is my mate?' An ant does the same and an elephant, a dog and even a hog do the same, day in and day out.

Eat, Sleep, Mate, Repeat: Is That It?

If we also centre our entire lives around how to eat, sleep, enjoy and repeat, how are we any better than a bird, an ant, a dog or a hog? There is only one purpose to the human life: to realize God and hence, realize our relationship with him. All our goals should be aligned with this one goal.

In order to help us realize and accomplish this goal of our lives, we need a Guru. If we have a problem understanding mathematics, we approach a maths teacher. If we are confused with some concept in chemistry, we seek the help of a chemistry teacher. In essence, to evolve our understanding of a particular subject, we approach an expert in that subject. Similarly, when it comes to understanding life and its complexities, a Guru is the perfect guide.

Human life only truly begins when we start working towards a higher purpose of God realization, and the person who helps us realize it, is known as a Guru.

Thus, every person, who considers themselves a human, must have a Guru. It is not an option.

tasmād guruṁ prapadyeta
jijñāsuḥ śreya uttamam

Shrimad Bhagavatam (11.3.2)

'A person who desires real happiness must seek a bona fide spiritual master and take shelter in him by initiation.'

Life is not a fairy tale, no matter how powerful, educated, young, old or knowledgeable we are. There will be times in life when we will find ourselves at crossroads, not knowing what to do. At these crucial moments, a Guru will guide us home.

Why Even Life Needs a Teacher

When we want to learn football, we immediately look for a coach, even though so many videos on 'How to play the sport' are available on internet. And while so much information about losing weight is doing the rounds in the market and on social media platforms, when we want to lose a few pounds, we approach a dietician or a nutritionist. Likewise, when we want to get educated, we turn away from the internet or the generic books available in the market, and seek a school and study from a teacher, who teaches us from authorized books.

But amazingly, when it comes to understanding life, people tend to think they know better and that they can understand or do things on their own. 'Whatever makes you feel good, just do it,' is a common response. Well, that's simply not how it works! Even the most knowledgeable are often confused about the questions that life throws at them every now and then. Thus, we must constantly keep ourselves under the guidance of a Guru, who is a true representative of God.

Even God, when He comes to this world to set an example for others, accepts a Guru. Think of Lord Krishna and how he considered Sandipani Muni as His Guru, or how Lord Ram accepted the sage Vishwamitra as His Guru.

A Guru Doesn't Kill Desires—He Aligns Them

A Guru's job is simple—he does not enter our lives to make us desireless but to purify our desires. Just like a powerful magnet instantly aligns the scattered iron filings in one line, a Guru helps us align our desires in the right direction to save us from the sufferings of the future. We are living a fast-paced life. A Guru enters our life and gives direction to this speed. He helps us reach our desired destination.

So . . . Who *Is* a Real Guru?

Now, a million-dollar question is: Who is a genuine Guru?

Being a good orator, or having a charismatic, popular personality or having a great following? None of these are the qualifications of a Guru, for these can be so easily faked.

The scriptures shed light on the subject. The Shrimad Bhagavatam (11.3.21) answers this:

> *śābde pare ca niṣṇātaṁ*
> *brahmaṇy upaśamāśrayam*

> 'The qualification of the bona fide guru is that he has realized the conclusions of the scriptures by deliberation and is able to convince others of these conclusions.'

A real Guru is someone who knows God and simply repeats His word, documented in the scriptures. He is a perfectly surrendered devotee of God, and his only duty is to guide people towards God. His sole purpose is to attract his followers towards God, not towards his own self. He is a transparent medium of mercy and the message of God. There is no other purpose of a Guru.

A guru is not someone who cures someone's disease or helps make profits in a business, nor should a Guru be approached for any such issues. He must only be sought to understand the purpose of life and how to achieve this purpose. His help should only be asked for if we are serious about making spiritual advancement. There should be no material motive.

How to *Find* a Real Guru? Desire

But how to find a real Guru?

All we have to do is desire. As soon as someone has a desire to connect with the Lord and seek answers to the questions of life, the Lord—residing as the Supersoul in our hearts—will start making wonderful arrangements to send one of His dearest servants into our lives as a Guru. Even if we are sitting in the remotest corner of the universe and suddenly develop an urge to understand God and His creation, the Lord will send a Guru—or we will be guided to one—who will hold our hand and lead us to God.

However, a word of caution here!

A person will enter our life as a Guru depending on how sincere or insincere our desire is. If our desires are superficial, say to simply flaunt a label of being 'spiritual' and to have something to say when we sit with our friends—'Oh, even I have a Guru whose weekly sessions I attend!'—or if we are not serious about the deeper understanding of our path, then a similar type of person will enter our life as a Guru.

He will make us feel that we are spiritual enough, but it will all be on a superficial level, and we will get nowhere forward on our path—even after listening to him for twenty years, we will have no understanding of God, our life and its purpose.

On the other hand, if we are sincere and serious about our spiritual life, an equally sincere, genuine representative of God will enter our life, guiding us at every step, purifying our hearts and getting us closer and closer to Him, filling our lives with utmost clarity, purpose and real happiness.

Thus, everything depends on our desire. If we wish to remain superficial, we will be cheated. If we are sincere, we will be more than rewarded.

Test. Then Trust

Once we come across a genuine Guru, we will still be allowed to test him by observing him. We will be allowed to ask a thousand questions. And once we are convinced and accept him as our Guru, then we should simply follow his course and have no doubts in our hearts. If we please the Guru, our God will be pleased. Likewise, if a Guru is displeased, God will be immensely displeased. Only by pleasing the Guru and by following his teachings will we make spiritual advancements. By the blessings of the Guru, even destiny can change, turning the impossible into possible.

mūkaṁ karoti vācālaṁ
paṅguṁ laṅghayate girim
yat-kṛpā tam ahaṁ vande
śrī-guruṁ dīna-tāraṇam
Chaitanya Charitamrita Madhya (17.80)

'By the mercy of the Guru, even a dumb man can become the greatest orator, and even a lame man can cross mountains.'

With a Guru's blessings, a person can achieve both material and spiritual success. Coming across a genuine Guru who is a true servant of God is considered to be the highlight of human life. Such an event marks the beginning of the end of all our miseries and opens the doors to immense good fortune in life, this and the ones that follow.

Thus, we must all sincerely desire and pray to Krishna to send one of His true representatives to hold our hand and help us reach His lotus feet.

3

We Are Spiritual Beings

The whole world is in the middle of an enormous crisis. And no, it's not the wars or terrorism or the growing mental health challenges. These are simply symptoms of a deeper issue: the identity crisis.

Everyone is busy identifying themselves as someone they are not and thus are occupied doing something that they are not supposed to do, resulting in chaos, both on the outside and on the inside. Imagine a situation where we have forgotten who we are. The result: we will end up knocking on doors to a house where we don't belong, doing things that shouldn't concern us, resulting in utter confusion for everyone. This is precisely what is happening at this moment.

Knocking on the Wrong Doors

People are narrowing their identities down to their nationality, gender, social or financial status, whereas the reality is that none of these are our true identities. People identifying themselves as Hindus, Muslims or Christians are fighting against each other for religious superiority. Men and women are fighting for control over each other, and the rich are busy trying to exert themselves as more evolved than the poor.

The conflicts all over the world are a result of this misidentification. We must realize that these are nothing but external, bodily designations, and these can change at any moment. Nationalities can change, genders can change and social status can bend as well. So how can these things contribute to our true identities?

A real identity does not change. And what is the real identity? It is that we are spiritual beings, spirit souls. We are not these material bodies. The body is constantly changing, and death is the final change after which we enter another body based on the actions of this life. As Krishna describes in the Bhagavad Gita (2.13):

dehino 'smin yathā dehe
kaumāraṁ yauvanaṁ jarā
tathā dehāntara-prāptir
dhīras tatra na muhyati

> 'As the embodied soul continuously passes, in this body, from boyhood to youth to old age, the soul similarly passes into another body at death. A sober person is not bewildered by such a change.'

Thus, the undue importance given to the body, and the things concerning this particular body, is absolute insanity. Negligence of our real self—the soul—is the root cause of all the chaos in our lives. Just by feeding the body, we cannot experience contentment in our lives. Just like food for the body, there is food for the soul, for the body is nothing but dead matter, active as long as the soul is present in it. As soon as the soul departs, this same body, which we spend so much time taking care of, becomes untouchable, demanding to be cremated at the earliest. What a sad end to something that we worked so hard to maintain or give comfort to, even at the cost of causing inconvenience to others, right? We have a body, but we are not this body.

Body = Vehicle, Soul = Driver

We are not this body, and life does not end with this body.

> *na tv evāhaṁ jātu nāsaṁ*
> *na tvaṁ neme janādhipāḥ*
> *na caiva na bhaviṣyāmaḥ*
> *sarve vayam ataḥ param*
>
> *Bhagavad Gita (2.12)*

> 'Lord Krishna: Never was there a time when I did not exist, nor you, nor all these kings; nor in the future shall any of us cease to be.'

The body is nothing but an external covering given to us based on our desires and karmas of past life. In truth, we are spirit souls, spiritual beings. Thus spiritual life is our natural life. And the more we live our natural life, the more peaceful our lives will be, irrespective of what happens around us.

That is not to say that we neglect this body completely. It is a fantastic vehicle using which we should perform actions to rectify the mistakes of our past, to build a better future. However, exclusive attention to the body, neglecting the needs of the soul, is thoroughly condemned.

A rich, old lady had a pet parrot. She deeply loved the parrot and took special care of its needs. Once, she went to the market and a beautiful cage made of pure gold caught her attention. She bought it, brought it home and put the parrot inside it, replacing the old cage.

She was so enamoured by the beauty of the cage that she would diligently polish it daily. This went on for a few days. Then one fine day, as she returned to perform her favourite task, to her utter shock, she found the parrot dead. That is when she realized her folly: In her fascination with the cage, she had forgotten to feed the bird, who eventually suffered and perished. What is the use of the cage without the bird?

Similarly, what is the use of the body if we neglect the soul? In our fascination with the body, we should not forget to feed the soul (our real self).

Out of Water: A Fish on Tour

Just like the natural environment of a fish is water—as soon as we take the fish away from water, it becomes restless. And even if we are to take this fish on a world tour, feeding it with the best of cuisines, the fish won't find respite and will eventually die. But as soon as the fish is brought back into the water, it becomes joyful, not in need of anything that we were trying to offer it in the first place.

Similarly, the more we stay connected to our natural environment, the more we shall be content and happy in life, irrespective of whether we have everything or nothing.

Once we understand that we are spirit souls or spiritual beings, parts and parcels of God, everything begins to make sense: Why should we pray? Why should we connect with God? Why must we chant His name? Why should we study scriptures?

Well, it's because that is where we belong. Our needs are spiritual. The body is only matter. A spiritual being trying to find happiness in matter is an incompatible situation. It is impossible. Anything that is matter or material will have a shelf life, a beginning and an end. Hence, no amount of material engagement will truly satisfy us.

Feed the Soul What It Craves

If we wish to experience everlasting happiness, we have to start finding joy in things that are of a similar nature to ours: spiritual. Just like a South Indian will find nourishment in South Indian food and a North Indian will find joy in North Indian cuisine, we will experience complete satisfaction in life when we eat food that is natural to us: spiritual. And what is the food for the soul?

The Soul is a speckle of God. When we regularly, as a daily discipline, chant the name of God—'*Hare Krishna, Hare Krishna, Krishna Krishna, Hare Hare/ Hare Rama, Hare Rama, Rama Rama, Hare Hare*'—worship His deity form and listen to His beautiful message from scriptures like the Bhagavad Gita, Shrimad Bhagavatam or Ramayana and associate with saintly people, the soul gets nourished and attains freedom from unnecessary lamentation or worries. Much like a hungry person, who feels completely pacified after having a fulfilling meal.

4

Tolerate the Change

A king got a beautiful ring made for himself. He wanted to inscribe something meaningful on it, so that whenever he felt sad, the inscription on the ring could make him happy; if he looked at the inscription in happiness, it would in turn make him feel solemn.

An announcement of the demand was made in the kingdom. Everyone got excited as whoever came up with the best suggestion for the inscription would be amply rewarded. Many pitched various ideas, but nothing satisfied the king—until one day he got what he wanted.

A man proposed: 'This too shall pass.' The king got the inscription done and, just as he had hoped for, the words made him feel better every time he was sad. Further, he would come back to being level-headed whenever he felt too overjoyed by things, simply by looking at the words on his ring and understanding the deep meaning they conveyed.

This too shall pass. Isn't this the secret to leading a happy life?

We live in a world where change is the only constant. We live in a world of duality, which means that wherever there is happiness, there will also be distress. If there is profit, sometimes life shall hand a loss, too. Similarly, there will be enemies if there are friends, and praise will always come hand in hand with criticism. Expect this duality of life and, more importantly, accept it.

Tolerate, Don't Agitate: The Gita's Formula for Resilience

According to Krishna, the only way to see through these changes is to tolerate them. He declares in the Bhagavad Gita (2.14):

mātrā-sparśās tu kaunteya
śītoṣṇa-sukha-duḥkha-dāḥ
āgamāpāyino 'nityās
tāṁs titikṣasva bhārata

'O son of Kunti, the impermanent appearance of happiness and distress and their disappearance in due course are like the appearance and disappearance of winter and summer seasons. They arise from sense perception, O scion of Bharata, and one must learn to tolerate them without being disturbed.'

There simply cannot be another way. We must tolerate both happiness and distress. By tolerating happiness, He cautions against becoming too proud, and in tolerating distress, He means not becoming overly sad. But how shall one tolerate?

1. By remembering that when we are going through distress, the stock of our bad karma is getting exhausted, thus making us mentally rejuvenated; and when we are experiencing joy, the stock of our good karma is getting exhausted, thus not letting us become complacent.
2. By remembering that neither happiness nor sorrow is permanent. If we are in the middle of a challenging time, it will pass; a happy situation won't last forever either.
3. By cultivating spiritual strength. Imagine that an enemy attacks us. If we are physically strong, we will easily be able to defend ourselves. However, physical strength doesn't always help in overcoming life's challenges. We need inner strength, which is synonymous to spiritual strength.

Build Inner Muscles: Why Spiritual Discipline Is Non-Negotiable

When we engage in regular, daily spiritual discipline by chanting God's name—'*Hare Krishna, Hare Krishna, Krishna Krishna, Hare Hare/Hare Rama, Hare Rama, Rama Rama, Hare Hare*'—and read spiritual literature like the Bhagavad Gita and Shrimad Bhagavatam, associate with saintly people as often as we can and worship the deity form of the Lord and Tulsi, we strengthen our inner muscles, which help to protect us from the onslaught of the inevitable, sudden changes in life.

These practices put us in a different zone, where we become immune to the things happening around us. Say, for example, we are standing outside our house on a hot, sunny day, with the temperature hovering around 45 degrees Celsius. Wouldn't it be extremely painful? Then, if we enter a room air-conditioned to 20 degrees Celsius, will we be affected by the heat anymore? No. But has the situation changed outside? Again, no. We are not affected because we are in a different environment.

Let us understand this with a better example. When on the runway while taking a flight, we see so many tall structures. The landscape could be overwhelming. But when we take off and go higher, the size of the buildings continues to become smaller, and beyond a certain point, the buildings seem too insignificant to even be visible. But they haven't truly disappeared from where they stood, it's just our perspective of things that doesn't make the landscape feel overwhelming anymore.

Similarly, we cannot alter the ever-changing nature of this world. No matter who we are, hardships will come sooner or later. It is the nature of hardships that isn't in our control. But whether we are affected or not is totally up to us. If we are well-prepared and internally strong, the hardships won't bother us, or at least the damage will be considerably minimized. Pain is inevitable; suffering, or the extent of it, is controllable.

Prepare in Peace, Survive in Storms

Unfortunately, when things are going well in life, we remain complacent and take them for granted. When situations suddenly change, we cannot cope with them. That's when we start running around, looking for the shelter of God, but the anxiety caused by the circumstances does not allow us to do that fully, either.

But remember: Those who sweat in peace, bleed less in war. Those who perform their spiritual practices when the time is good will find it easy to manage things, compared to others, when things go bad. There is no way around it. We must take our spiritual life seriously, and we will find it much easier to sail through and see the other side of any kind of challenges.

5

The Temporary Outfit

Once, a criminal, having committed a crime, was running away from the police. He entered a particular house, changed his clothes and came out. To his utter surprise, the police still caught him. He questioned, 'How did you arrest me? I committed the crime wearing a different set of clothes. This is a different outfit.' The police replied, 'Why should we care about what clothes you wore earlier? We are concerned with the person inside this dress. He is the culprit.'

So often, we find people questioning the reasons behind their suffering. Is it something to do with the actions of their past lives, of which they don't even remember anything about? Well, here is the answer.

The body is simply an outer garment of the soul, our real self as the Bhagavad Gita (2.22) explains:

vāsāṁsi jīrṇāni yathā vihāya
navāni gṛhṇāti naro 'parāṇi
tathā śarīrāṇi vihāya jīrṇāny
anyāni saṁyāti navāni dehī

'As a person puts on new garments, giving up old ones, the soul similarly accepts new material bodies, giving up the old and useless ones.'

Three Layers, One Self

In fact, we have three bodies:

1. The gross body (made of earth, water, fire, air and ether), which we can see with our naked eye
2. The subtle body, consisting of the mind, its intelligence and false ego
3. The spiritual body (the soul, the real you)

In essence, we are covered with two types of garments: one gross and one subtle.

When a person dies, the gross body is left behind and cremated. The subtle body carries the soul to the next destination based on the impressions, experiences and desires stored in the mind.

We are the same, original person in different types of bodies, living through different lives. So, if we engage in wrongful acts, their results will come at an appropriate time. It could be in this life or the next.

The body is dead matter and has no power of its own. It is only the soul acting through it. Thus, even if the body changes, the original person, the soul, remains the same, which must bear the fruit of its actions, irrespective of where it is. The laws of karma take into consideration not just this lifetime but all lifetimes.

Human by Body, Human by Qualities?

This fact also highlights another very important principle in life:

Just by putting on the uniform of a lawyer or a doctor, a person does not become these people. He must qualify as one. Similarly, just by being bestowed with the body of a human, one does not become a human being. As mentioned earlier, the body is simply a temporary, outer garment for the soul. To be considered a human being, a person needs to qualify as one.

And what is that qualification?

The Vedanta Sutra (1.1.1) says:

athāto brahma jijñāsā

'Now that you have got this human body, let us enquire about God: "brahma" (the absolute truth).'

Further, it is stated in the Hitopadesha 25:

āhāra-nidrā-bhaya-maithunaṁ ca
sāmānyam etat paśubhir narāṇām
dharmo hi teṣām adhiko viśeṣo
dharmeṇa hīnaḥ paśubhiḥ samānaḥ

'Eating, sleeping, bodily enjoyment (sex life) and defence—these four principles are common to both human beings and animals. The distinction between human life and animal life is that a man can search for God (his real dharma or duty) but an animal cannot. If a human being is not working towards this higher goal, he is no better than an animal.'

It is not an abusive statement. It is common sense and simply stating the facts. For example, if we see someone acting like a monkey, we call him a monkey. If we see someone eating anything and everything, we say the person is hogging (or eating like a hog). This clearly implies that a person is known by his acts, and not by his external appearances.

Similarly, if a person's life only remains centred around the four basic propensities of eating, sleeping, mating and defending, how is he better than an animal?

We are truly considered a human being only when we stop living a whimsical life based on what we feel and think is right, and start leading a God-conscious life, in accordance with His will and laws. And, for this, we need the constant teachings of a Guru.

The mother gives birth to the body of a human, but it is the Guru who—by creating a strong spiritual foundation—makes us a human being and thus connects us with God.

Desire Determines Destination

Desire is the key to a better life; the mindset is the key. If we desire to attend a birthday party, we end up dressing for the occasion, and if we wish to attend a prayer meet, a more sober dress is arranged for. In a similar manner, if we wish to have a better body in the next life, we must lead a God-conscious life now. Only then, if not a spiritual body, at least a human body is guaranteed; not just the body of an ordinary human being, but a blessed being.

If we only care about eating, sleeping, mating and defending what we have, we will be granted a degraded body in lower species. The body is given based on the type of desires the soul cultivates. If our desire is only to eat, drink and be merry, and not care about the higher purpose of life—which is an endeavour to make spiritual advancement—then the authorities of the universe might think, 'All right, if you simply wish to enjoy, why waste a human body? Let us give you a suitable animal body, where you can enjoy without any accountability for your actions.'

Animals can only live their karma. They have no means to rectify it. Since they lack this potential, they are also not held responsible for their actions. The danger, though, is that once the soul gets trapped into the lower species of life, it has to go through the entire cycle of eighty-four lakh species of life before attaining a human body again.

The Rare Gift: Make It Count

Just imagine how rare it is to be born as a human. Out of 8.4 million species, only the human form is endowed with the gift of conscious decision-making, the ability to question existence and the intelligence to seek the higher truth. This human life is not just an accident of nature—it is a golden opportunity granted after countless lifetimes of evolution through various species.

We, as humans, are uniquely blessed with the power to choose—to rise above instinct and live with intention. And with this power comes responsibility. Unlike animals, whose actions are governed by instinct alone, we are held accountable for our thoughts, actions and desires. Our choices become seeds, and those seeds bear fruit—either uplifting us to higher realms or binding us to lower births.

So the question is not just what we are doing, but why we are doing it, and for whom. Are we living just to please our senses, or are we living to purify our soul? Are we drifting through life unconsciously, or are we walking a deliberate path toward our eternal home?

If we truly desire a better future—not only in this life, but in the life beyond—we must align our desires with our eternal nature. A God-centered life is not a life of restriction, but a life of liberation. It is the life where we begin to remember who we really are: not a fleeting body, but an immortal soul, part and parcel of the Divine.

Let us not waste this rare human birth chasing fleeting shadows. Instead, let us live purposefully, act responsibly, and love unconditionally, all while keeping God at the center. For it is only in that alignment that we fulfill the true potential of this temporary outfit—and move closer to our eternal identity.

6

Born to Die, Bound to Live

Once, during his travels, a saint reached a village where he found a woman who was crying and lamenting the loss of her son. She ran around frantically, requesting anyone and everyone to help her, hoping for a miracle that would revive her son. Her heart filled with renewed hope when she saw the saint. She fell at his feet and pleaded, 'Please bring my son back to life. I cannot live without him. How and why did he leave me? This is not fair.'

The saint listened, smiled and told her, 'All right, I will revive your son. But I need a palmful of rice to make this happen.' The lady was overjoyed at the prospect and immediately agreed to do the needful. But the saint added, 'There is one condition, though. This rice must come from a house where no death has ever taken place. Only then will it work.'

The lady rushed to a house in the immediate vicinity. When she asked for a palmful of rice, the family members living there immediately agreed to give it to her. But when they heard the saint's condition, they humbly excused themselves from helping the lady as so many deaths had taken place in the family lineage in the past.

The lady knocked on the next door, only for the same story to repeat. She visited all the homes in the village but could not find a single house where no death had ever taken place.

Gradually, it dawned upon her that death was among the most common things in all households. It was a harsh reality of life that no one wanted to discuss or think about, but also the one that nobody could avoid. Death wasn't unusual. This acceptance brought her a sense of peace.

She returned to the saint and thanked him for manifesting this realization in her. He smiled and told her how death was inevitable to everyone who was born.

The One Truth No One Escapes

No matter who we are, we cannot escape death. The moment we are born, we also begin dying. If we are forty years old, it means forty years of our life is finished, or we have died for forty years. The Bhagavad Gita (2.27) emphatically reiterates this truth:

jātasya hi dhruvo mṛtyur
dhruvaṁ janma mṛtasya ca
tasmād aparihārye 'rthe
na tvaṁ śocitum arhasi

'One who has taken his birth is sure to die, and after death one is sure to take birth again. Therefore, in the unavoidable discharge of your duty, you should not lament.'

With every rise and set, the sun reduces everyone's life duration by one day. It's ironic how every day we hear of so many deaths and still live with a stupid belief that we may never die. We become so deeply engrossed in our materialistic pursuits that we forget this reality of life, and when it does strike us or our near and dear ones, we are shattered.

Therefore, it is very important to constantly read the scriptures, and associate oneself with saintly people, whose wisdom works as a reminder, keeping us grounded and ever so conscious of the laws this world is governed by—one of the most prominent ones of which is (Bhagavad Gita [2.27]):

'Anyone who is born is sure to die and anyone who has died, is sure to be born again.'

What Are We Really Running After?

It is important to sometimes contemplate death. Many yogis are sometimes seen meditating on funeral pyres (burning dead bodies) just to keep themselves reminded of the inevitable end of this body we try so hard to maintain, neglecting the needs of our true self, the soul.

Simultaneously, it helps us to cultivate reasonable detachment from our materialistic lives. An intelligent person would think, 'What am I running after every day? Just for the comfort and enjoyment of this body, I waste so much of my valuable time taking immoral ways to earn, exploiting the innocent and sometimes I even cultivate enmity with others. It will be finished one day. When? I do not know. It could be the very next moment, tomorrow or sometime later. But it will surely be gone. And in the process of trying to protect and enjoy something temporary, I am spoiling my future. Why not try to make the best use of the bad bargain? Why not use this temporary body for some permanent gain?'

As long as this body is alive, we must utilize it to serve others to make their lives better. And, most importantly, serve God to make our own life, the present one and the next, better. The only things that go with us at the time of death are the fruits of our actions.

Our actions decide our next body, family, place of birth and every other aspect of future existence. Even though we try to hold on to this body, it is deteriorating every day and it will fully perish one day. After that, it either becomes food for the vultures or transforms to dust and turns into ashes. However, since the soul is eternal, with the end of the body, our existence does not end.

> *na tv evāhaṁ jātu nāsaṁ*
> *na tvaṁ neme janādhipāḥ*
> *na caiva na bhaviṣyāmaḥ*
> *sarve vayam ataḥ param*
>
> *Bhagavad Gita* (2.12)

> Lord Krishna said: 'Never was there a time when I did not exist, nor you, nor all these kings; nor in the future shall any of us cease to be.'

The Soul Never Dies—Only the Dress Changes

After death, we simply take up another body based on our actions and thoughts in the previous life. A rebirth is sure to happen, whether as a higher life or a lower is decided by the authorities of the universe that carefully examine our past actions.

Death is not something to be scared of. If our house becomes unfit for living, we change the house. If our clothes become old, we change them. Similarly, our body is simply a house or a garment for the soul.

When this body becomes unfit for living, we change our body to a new one. As long as we have the present body, let us speak and act in a way that prepares a better future body for us. Every action performed and every word spoken is like a seed sown, which will then give fruit in future, either as happiness or distress. The type of fruit will depend on the type of seed. Let us be careful and, at the same time, joyful.

From Birth to Death—Make the Right 'C' Choice

When a death happens, instead of lamenting too much, we must engage in actions that would help in the onward journey of the soul. Chanting or singing the holy names of Krishna and reciting the sacred Bhagavad Gita and especially the Shrimad Bhagavatam, are the activities that not only help the soul attain liberation but also build an environment of positivity and enormous hope around us.

Life is a journey from 'B' (birth) to 'D' (death). But between 'B' and 'D' comes 'C', which stands for choices. We are the products of our choices. Let us make the right choices if we want a bright future: immediately and most essentially, in the long term.

7

Bhakti Yoga

We Only Stand to Gain

Material activities and their results end with the body. But the spiritual credits acquired by serving Krishna (God) are never lost and stay with the person, life after life. Even if a person has done little on the path of Bhakti Yoga (devotional service), he is sure to have a chance of being born again as a human being in the next life, either in the family of a great devotional culture, or in a rich aristocratic family that will give him a further chance to make spiritual progress. Lord Krishna gives this greatest hope in the Bhagavad Gita (2.40):

nehābhikrama-nāśo 'sti
pratyavāyo na vidyate

sv-alpam apy asya dharmasya
trāyate mahato bhayāt

'In this endeavour, there is no loss or diminution, and a little advancement on this path can protect one from the most dangerous type of fear.'

Spiritual Effort Is Never Wasted

Even a small beginning of spiritual activity finds no impediment, nor can that small beginning be lost at any stage. Any work begun on the material plane has to be completed; otherwise, the whole attempt becomes a failure. But any work begun in Krishna's service has a permanent effect, even if not finished.

The devotee of Krishna is therefore not at a loss even if his work in bhakti is incomplete. One per cent done in Krishna's service bears permanent results, so that the next beginning is from the point of 2 per cent; whereas in material activity, without 100 per cent success there is no profit.

Also, whatever little we have done in devotional service to Krishna, the spiritual credits acquired will save us from the gravest dangers in life, which may otherwise manifest and snowball into something graver as a result of our previous karmas.

Unintentional Devotion, Eternal Effect

The Shrimad Bhagavatam (Chapters 1–3) tells one such episode of a young boy named Ajamila, who although extremely pious, religious, pure, respectful and humble, fell down due to association with a prostitute.

He kicked out his pure and simple-hearted wife from a respectable family, neglected his old parents and spent the rest of his time enjoying life with the prostitute. When his wealth ran out, he began stealing, gambling, and even robbing people only to please her and satisfy her demands. In this way, he spent eighty-eight years of his life sinning, until one day, the moment of his death arrived. As he lay on his deathbed, he suddenly saw three scary people, ropes around their shoulders, staring at him. They were the Yamadutas, messengers of Yamaraj, the Lord of death.

They had come to take the sinful Ajamila to their master, intending to punish him on account of his sins. They tied up Ajamila with their ropes, and out of great fear, Ajamila called out to his youngest son, Narayan, who was playing close by.

'Narayan! Narayan!' he said.

As soon as the name came out of his mouth, the entire room, which was pitch dark until then, suddenly lit up as four effulgent personalities, messengers of Lord Narayan, appeared on the scene.

They cut the ropes binding Ajamila's soul and forbade the Yamadutas from taking him away. When questioned by the Yamadutas as to why they were trying to save a sinful soul, the messengers of Lord Narayan emphatically declared that by chanting the holy name of Narayan in a helpless state—even though he was addressing his son, he uttered the Lord's name nonetheless—Ajamila was now free from not just the sins of this life but those of the previous lives as well.

Thus, Ajamila was saved and bestowed a second chance. A calamity as big as death was averted by a little devotional service done unconsciously. But what did Ajamila do to deserve this saving grace?

It is important to note that as a child, Ajamila worshipped Lord Narayan sincerely. Later, as he grew addicted to a sinful lifestyle, he gave up his worship. But the merciful Lord did not forget his service. He was always on a lookout for an opportunity to save his beloved disciple and inspired him to name his son after Him: Narayan.

Power of the Holy Name—Even if Chanted Jokingly

When nothing else works, the name of the Lord, endowed with all his blessings and power, certainly does. Ajamila was too impure to hear and assimilate any moral and spiritual instructions. The only way out, the Lord thought, was if somehow, he could be made to chant His holy name. Thus, he made his arrangements and got Ajamila's son named after Him. Hence, every time Ajamila addressed his son, he was getting freed from his sinful karmas.

sāṅketyaṁ pārihāsyaṁ vā
stobhaṁ helanam eva vā
vaikuṇṭha-nāma-grahaṇam
aśeṣāgha-haraṁ viduḥ

Shrimad Bhagavatam (6.2.14)

'One who chants the holy name of the Lord is immediately freed from the reactions of unlimited sins, even if he chants indirectly [to indicate something else], jokingly, for musical entertainment, or even neglectfully. This is accepted by all the learned scholars of the scriptures.'

patitaḥ skhalito bhagnaḥ
sandaṣṭas tapta āhataḥ
harir ity avaśenāha
pumān nārhati yātanāḥ

Shrimad Bhagavatam (6.2.15)

'If one chants the holy name of Hari and then dies because of an accidental misfortune, such as falling from the top of a house, slipping and suffering broken bones while travelling on the road, being bitten by a serpent, being afflicted with pain and high fever, or being injured by a weapon, one is immediately absolved from having to enter hellish life, even though he is sinful.'

gurūṇāṁ ca laghūnāṁ ca
gurūṇi ca laghūni ca
prāyaścittāni pāpānāṁ
jñātvoktāni maharṣibhiḥ

Shrimad Bhagavatam (6.2.16)

'Authorities who are learned scholars and sages have carefully ascertained that one should atone for the heaviest sins by undergoing a heavy process of atonement and one should atone for lighter sins by undergoing lighter atonement. Chanting the Hare Krishna mantra, however, vanquishes all the effects of sinful activities, regardless of whether heavy or light.'

Thus, the path of Bhakti Yoga, beginning with hearing and chanting the holy name, fame, qualities and pastimes of the Lord, is the easiest, quickest, safest and surest path to perfection. It is a path on which we can run blindly and even if we fall down after some time, there is no loss.

tyaktvā sva-dharmaṁ caraṇāmbujaṁ harer
bhajann apakvo 'tha patet tato yadi

yatra kva vābhadram abhūd amuṣya kiṁ
ko vārtha āpto 'bhajatāṁ sva-dharmataḥ
Shrimad Bhagavatam (1.5.17)

'If someone gives up his occupational duties and engages in Krishna's devotional service and then falls down before completing his spiritual journey, what loss is there on his part? And what can one gain if one performs his material activities perfectly?'

Or, as the Christians say, 'What profiteth a man if he gains the whole world yet suffers the loss of his eternal soul?'

What if I Try Bhakti and Fail?

Whatever progress we have made will become our eternal asset and will save us from the most dangerous kinds of fears. It is so simple that even a child can take part in it. A child cannot follow the path of karma, dhyana or yoga, but he can certainly sing the names of the Lord and worship His deity with flowers, fruit or some water.

Even if we cannot do anything, if we cannot read scriptures, cannot understand the philosophy, if our behaviour is not up to the standard and still if we simply offer obeisances before the deity, we will undoubtedly make spiritual progress.

If we go to the temple and offer respects to the deity, play musical instruments during *kirtan* (devotional singing), get some fruit or flowers for the Lord or offer some monetary service, everything will be taken into account by Krishna and repaid with interest at a moment when we need it the most.

Simply put, good karma does not nullify bad karma. Only devotional karma does. Thus, real intelligence means investing our time, energy and resources in things that will yield permanent benefits, life after life, and the path of Bhakti Yoga stands supreme among all in this regard.

8

Duty vs Detachment

One of the most profound teachings of the Bhagavad Gita is encapsulated in Chapter 2, Verse 47:

> *karmaṇy evādhikāras te*
> *mā phaleṣu kadācana*
> *mā karma-phala-hetur bhūr*
> *mā te saṅgo 'stv akarmaṇi*

> 'You have a right to perform your prescribed duty, but you are not entitled to the fruits of action. Never consider yourself the cause of the results of your activities and never be attached to not doing your duty.'

This verse strikes at the very core of human anxiety—our attachment to results. From the moment we begin any endeavour, our minds become preoccupied with the outcome: 'Will I succeed? Will I be rewarded? Will I get recognition?' This attachment to results creates fear, worry and disappointment.

We often believe that we can control what happens in our lives. We make plans, put in effort and expect specific results. But the reality is that outcomes are shaped by countless factors beyond our control.

Effort Isn't Everything

No farmer can force the harvest to grow; he can only till the land, sow the seeds and nurture the crops. Whether the rains will come or whether pests will destroy the yield is not in his hands.

Similarly, we may work hard at a job, invest time in relationships or strive toward a goal, but external circumstances influence what actually happens. A musician can compose and perform beautifully, but whether the audience appreciates it is not in his hands. A student may study diligently, but unforeseen circumstances may affect the exam results. When we pin our happiness on results, we subject ourselves to constant highs and lows, dictated by circumstances that we cannot govern.

The Five Hidden Forces Behind Every Outcome

Krishna's wisdom reminds us of a liberating truth—we are only responsible for our actions, not their outcomes.

Why does Krishna say so? There are two main reasons:

1. Because there are other factors, apart from our efforts, that are responsible for the accomplishment of any action.

These are five in number:

a. The person
b. The place of the action
c. The effort (hard work)
d. The destiny, and
e. The will of God

Generally, we hear that hard work is the key to success and when a person achieves success in any endeavour, he considers himself to be the doer, thus taking all the credit.

This is a sign of a big false ego, as here, we clearly see that our effort is just one of the factors coming in to accomplish an action. Many times, we see a person working hard but still remaining far from success. This is due to other factors not being in his favour.

Destiny is bigger than our efforts. Even if we are the right person, at the right place and with right amount of endeavour, but if something is not in our destiny, we will not get it. But then, shall we simply surrender to destiny? Not at all.

Grace Is Greater

The fifth factor, the will or grace of God, is bigger than even destiny. If somehow, God's will is in our favour, our destiny will change and we will achieve whatever it is we desire, or do not even deserve. God has the ultimate say in all matters. A prisoner inside the prison cell has no ability to get out on his own. But the head of the state can order his release easily. This is an example of grace. He is destined to suffer for, say ten years, but due to the mercy shown by the higher authority, he is released much earlier. Thus leading a God-conscious life is our only saving grace. Our efforts and His grace is the perfect combination to accomplish things.

2. Krishna wants us to rise beyond selfishness. He is like a loving father who prepares his child for a practical and sacred approach towards life.

Not everything should be done expecting something in return. God is the ultimate enjoyer of all the fruits of our actions. Without His will, we cannot even breathe, forget about achieving things in life. All the credit is His alone. We must offer the fruits of our actions to Him, but that does not mean we shouldn't enjoy the sense of our accomplishments.

Think of it like the clouds taking water from the water bodies during summer, and during the rainy season, returning this water in abundance. Similarly, we offer the fruit of our actions to God, who then returns the enjoyment in the form of happiness in abundance. This happiness is free from any karmic reaction because it is on a spiritual realm. If we try to enjoy the fruit of our actions, we get more and more stuck in the karmic processes, for everything we do has a reaction. Life should not remain centred around 'I, me, and mine'. It is meant for a higher purpose: selfless service to God and all His children in this world.

Real Joy Comes from Selfless Service

Only when a person does something selflessly does he actually experience true happiness and contentment in life. The more we expect and want to enjoy rewards in exchange for what we do, the more we prepare ourselves for misery. Detachment from the result is the key to happiness. This does not mean we just work with no result in mind. It means we do our best and then whatever be the result, we accept it and continue performing our duties.

We shouldn't be complacent when we get what we desire, and we shouldn't get depressed if we do not get what we want. The only way to save oneself from distress is to work in a selfless manner, whether or not the result of our actions is to our liking.

Life is not a fairy tale where we always get what we want. Sometimes we do and sometimes we do not. We have to rise above these unrealistic expectations of wanting things to go our way all the time. The sooner we begin to perform our actions as a duty, without being attached to the result, the more peaceful we become.

Only when we perform '*nishkam*-karma', that is an action without expecting anything in return, do we really evolve to a higher moral and spiritual level.

9

Sense Control

Taming the Wild Within

In a world that constantly pulls us in a thousand directions, where desires whisper temptations and distractions cloud our focus, true intelligence is not merely about knowledge—it is about control. The Bhagavad Gita reveals a timeless secret: mastery over life begins with mastery over the senses. Lord Krishna declares in the Bhagavad Gita (2.61):

tāni sarvāṇi saṁyamya
yukta āsīta mat-paraḥ
vaśe hi yasyendriyāṇi
tasya prajñā pratiṣṭhitā

'One who restrains his senses, keeping them under full control, and fixes his consciousness upon Me, is known as a man of steady intelligence.'

The Epidemic of Instant Gratification

'Just do it' seems to have become the cardinal principle for the people of this generation. If something makes you feel good or happy, just do it, wherein instant gratification seems to be the goal. No one seems to be considering right or wrong. There is no differentiation. If everyone is doing something, it is accepted as the right thing to do, even if it is sinful.

This is due to a lack of control over the senses, which, in turn, is driving us crazy. The eyes want to see something nice, the ears want to hear something sweet or controversial, the tongue wants to speak uselessly and taste palatable things, the skin wants to touch something soft and the nose gets enamoured by a nice fragrance.

Since we do whatever our senses want and whenever they want, we are not able to live in peace. The more we give in to the demands of our senses, the more addicted we become to these demands. Sometimes, we tend to think that, by doing everything our senses crave for, we will get done with the craving and then will never again feel tempted. The truth, though, is that fulfilling the demands of our senses is like adding fuel to fire. The fire only grows bigger. Uncontrolled senses drive a person crazy, who then loses the ability to differentiate between right and wrong and is willing to do anything just to fulfil his sensory cravings.

The Chariot of Life

Imagine a chariot being driven by five horses. The horses are supposed to drive the chariot to the destination. They will do so if the reins are held tight by the charioteer. If the reins are loose, all five horses will run in different directions, bewildering the passenger sitting on the chariot and never allowing him to reach his desired destination.

Similarly, our five senses are like these five horses, the chariot is the body and the reins are the mind; the chariot driver, who is supposed to guide the vehicle through the horses, is the intelligence. If we do not use our intelligence to differentiate between what to be done and what is not to be done and allow our senses to indulge in whatever they like, we will forever be lost in life and will never be able to focus on anything. But then, what do we do? Must we stop having any fun in life? Not at all.

Regulation, Not Repression

As long as we have senses, they do need some gratification or enjoyment. Enjoyment is not forbidden, but it must be regulated. Since we are blessed with the ability to make choices, we are bound to be held responsible for the choices we make. Thus, it is important we choose carefully—what we eat, how we speak and the things we do.

With every choice, we sow a seed of happiness or distress for the future. But how shall we know what is right and what is not? The common notion is that if everyone does it, it must be right, isn't it? Well, the majority do not always decide the truth. The right thing will still be right, even if no one does it, and the wrong deed will always be wrong, even if everyone does it.

Truth Is Not a Popularity Contest

Once, a man went to a court where a criminal was being tried for a serious crime. He requested the judge, 'My Lord, please set this man free. He is innocent.'

The judge asked, 'What makes you say that?'

The man replied, 'Well, all the people seated in this courtroom, including me, feel so. All the people outside the court, and even the newspapers say so, too. Since everyone feels he is innocent, he must be freed.'

The judge replied, 'You may feel or say whatever you wish to, but the judgment will be passed based on the books of the law.'

Similarly, irrespective of what we feel or what others say, we will only be judged for our actions based on what is right or what is wrong in the books of the law—our scriptures. The scriptures emphatically mention how we must regulate the activities of our senses and not indulge them indiscriminately, otherwise there will be serious karmic repercussions in the form of mental distress, legal complications, chronic diseases, disappointments, setbacks and failures in life.

This is similar to a person breaking the laws of the state and receiving punishment in return.

The Four Pitfalls of the Pleasure-Seeker

The four sinful activities that we must never allow our senses if we wish to live happily are: meat eating, intoxication (of any kind), illicit affairs and gambling. These four are the pillars of a sinful life, and anyone who engages in these acts will suffer, sooner or later.

Just because the repercussions are not immediate does not mean they will never come. There is a reason karma is compared to a seed. When we sow a seed, we do not see the fruit immediately for it fructifies at the right time. Time separates an individual from his karmic repercussions, but the reaction is sure to come in the forms mentioned above.

Just like a person who lives under the rules and regulations set by the government lives in peace, a person living under the regulations laid down by God, and mentioned in the scriptures, will have both physical and mental prosperity.

But then, Krishna also says in the Bhagavad Gita (2.60):

yatato hy api kaunteya
puruṣasya vipaścitaḥ
indriyāṇi pramāthīni
haranti prasabhaṁ manaḥ

'The senses are so strong and impetuous, O Arjuna, that they forcibly carry away the mind even of a man of discrimination who is endeavouring to control them.'

Then, how do we control our senses?

In two ways:

1. Avoid contemplation:
   We cannot avoid our senses coming in touch with sense objects. There is so much material available all day long. However, what we can avoid is contemplating the object the senses have perceived. Do not think about it. Resist the temptation.

However, on most occasions, when we forcibly try to resist things, the resistance does not last long.

Then what do we do?

2. Give them a superior taste/better engagement:

As mentioned in the Bhagavad Gita (2.59):

viṣayā vinivartante
nirāhārasya dehinaḥ
rasa-varjaṁ raso 'py asya
paraṁ dṛṣṭvā nivartate

'Though the embodied soul may be restricted from sensory enjoyment, the temptations remain. What needs to be fixed is the consciousness, and a way to do it is by engaging in and experiencing superior taste.'

Don't Resist. Redirect

If we keep trying to control our senses by telling ourselves, 'I should not eat this, or I should not look at something, maybe I should not listen to that,' it may work a few times, but a resistance of this kind won't last forever. After a point, we fall prey to the temptations. The solution is to give our senses something better to engage with, something so attractive that they forget the engagements of a lower nature. This is similar to a naughty child being told by his parents to stop being naughty and sit in one place. The child will only act according to the nature of a child; he may sit quietly for a while, but soon enough, he will find a way to make mischief. The solution is to engage him in a better, more constructive activity, which is engaging enough to make him forget the mischief he is so prone to making.

In essence, when we employ:

1. Our sense of sight: the eyes must seek the graceful form of Krishna
2. Our sense of hearing: the ears must listen to beautiful narrations of Him from our scriptures
3. Our sense of touch: it should be to serve His deity form, in contacting with things that are sacred to Him
4. Our sense of smell: the nose must smell flowers, incense, Tulsi leaves, everything that constitutes the fragrance of Him; and
5. Our sense of palate or taste: the tongue must taste the food offered to Him; it must chant His holy name

Only then do our senses gain a higher taste, which protects them from getting attracted to the lower tastes of this world.

The Goal of Sense Control

Why does a doctor ask his patient to stop eating for a while, or only eat specific food? Because the patient is in bad health owing to unhealthy eating habits. The ultimate goal is to not stop him from eating, but to nurse him back to normal health so he can enjoy regular food. In the same manner, when scriptures or saintly people talk about controlling our senses, it is because our senses are attached to the wrong things, and the goal is to engage them with the right things. Unless we stop them from one engagement, how can we engage them elsewhere?

Krishna is Rishikesha, the master of the senses. If He is the master, then obviously our senses are the servants, and thus are meant to be engaged in serving Him. A servant is happy as long as he serves his master faithfully. As soon as he tries to be independent of the will of his master, his problems begin. We are spiritual beings, parts and parcels of God. Therefore, engaging our senses in the service of God (Krishna) is the only healthy state of our senses.

A person whose senses are engaged in devotional service to Krishna does not need sensory control because the goal of this control is already accomplished. The senses are engaged where they should be.

The senses need engagement—whether inferior (material) or superior (spiritual), the choice is ours. Depending on how we utilize them, we invite future happiness or misery into our lives. They are a great asset and must be utilized to create a better future, immediate and long term (next life).

The Smart King

Once, a sailor aboard a ship was going across the ocean to sell his goods. Suddenly, he encountered a storm, and his boat capsized. Somehow, after a lot of struggles, he managed to swim across to an island. As he stepped onto the island, he thanked the Lord for saving his life but remained uncertain about his future. He saw a group of people running towards him with their hands raised. They shouted, 'Long live the king, long live the king!' The man looked to his left and to his right for a glimpse of the king, but he found no one. He realised the people were shouting for him.

He wondered, 'How can I be the king? I could barely manage to escape death!' But he decided to go with the flow, and asked the strangers, the inhabitants of that island, 'Am I your king?' With a big smile on their faces, they responded, 'Yes, you are the king.'

They picked him up, put him on a palanquin and, joyfully singing and dancing, carried him to the local palace where he was enthroned as the king of the island. The man started living his life in great happiness until one day, his minister informed him, 'O dear king, on this island, a person can be the king only for five years. Once this duration gets over, those same people who picked you up near the ocean and brought you here will pick you up again, mercilessly carry you and throw you into a deep, dark forest infested with demons and wild beasts, where you will die a miserable death.'

The king was horrified, but he was intelligent. He thought things over and called the minister over to him. He whispered something in the minister's ear. Hearing what the king said, the minister expressed his disapproval and responded that it was not possible.

The king ordered, 'You better get going. If you do not accomplish this task, remember, I am still the king and I will cut off your head, and you will die a miserable death.'

The minister had no other option and immediately left to complete the task. After five years, the inhabitants of the island came again, but this time, their welcoming smile was gone and was replaced by a symbolic, demonic mischief in their eyes.

They picked the king up and carried him to the forest where they had thrown many kings in the past, but to their surprise, they saw that no forest remained. It was replaced by a flourishing kingdom, inhabited by wonderful people, surrounded by beautiful lakes and gardens and decorated with beautiful, most enchanting palaces. Puzzled, they looked at the king, who smiled at them and invited them over to live in the new palace with him. They lived happily ever after.

This is an interesting story that also gives us a very important and pertinent lesson. The island or the kingdom in the story refers to our body. Our soul is the king, the owner of this kingdom. The minister refers to the senses, and the inhabitants who picked up the king to bring him to the throne and to throw him into the forest refer to our near and dear ones. The five years duration of the king's tenure in the kingdom refers to the limited duration of life that we all have. The beautiful kingdom that replaces the forest refers to the spiritual realm, a higher destination, a better future.

The Real Investment Plan

The king's intelligence lay in recognizing his limited time in the kingdom, after which he was going to be forced to leave. He decided to utilize this time to prepare for a better future. He ordered the minister to turn that wild forest into a beautiful kingdom, so that when his rule came to an end, he would have a better place to live. Similarly, the duration of our life is also fixed. No matter how much we enjoy this time, the truth is we cannot enjoy it forever. One day, we must leave and go elsewhere. But where? Nobody has an answer to that. But just like the king, we must utilize our senses to prepare for a better destination.

We do not know when that last moment will come, but in whatever time we are left with, we must try to make the right choices ,for only that ensures a better life and a future of happiness. In this life, we must prepare for a better next life.

This is real intelligence. We are busy investing in property, banks, stocks or mutual funds, but none of these things matter once we die. We must invest in the afterlife, too. The more we become conscious of this aspect in life, more responsible human beings we shall become.

10

Desires

The Silent Dictators

We are the products of our own desires. We are constantly being bombarded with unlimited ones. The usual tendency is to immediately act upon them with the hope that fulfilling them will bring peace and put an end to our hankerings. Well, Krishna does not agree with this thought. He says:

āpūryamāṇam acala-pratiṣṭhaṁ
samudram āpaḥ praviśanti yadvat
tadvat kāmā yaṁ praviśanti sarve
sa śāntim āpnoti na kāma-kāmī

Bhagavad Gita (2.70)

> 'A person who is not disturbed by the incessant flow of desires—that enter like rivers into the ocean, which is ever being filled but is always still—can alone achieve peace, and not the man who strives to satisfy such desires.'

Trying to fulfil every desire of our mind will not satisfy the heart but tolerating it certainly will. The nature of material desires is such that as soon as one gets fulfilled, it gives birth to another one. It's a vicious, never-ending cycle.

But every time we tolerate a temptation, we become stronger, and the next time we face a similar temptation, we will have greater strength to battle it. Every time we give in, we grow weaker.

How Does One Tolerate Desires?

Krishna gives a beautiful example of an ocean. The desires entering our hearts are like the rivers entering the ocean.

During summer, gallons of water evaporate from the ocean, but the ocean remains unaffected. During monsoon, gallons of water get poured into the ocean, but it still remains unfettered. In addition, each and every river ends up in the ocean, but the ocean remains unbothered.

On the other hand, think of a puddle of water. The rains fill it up instantly, and the sun dries it out in no time. It's because the puddle lacks depth. The ocean is unaffected because it is deep. Likewise, a person's ability to tolerate grows with spiritual depth. This spiritual depth is synonymous to inner strength.

So, we must act on two levels: try to resist temptations and, simultaneously, go deeper into our spiritual life, which will further increase our ability to resist the unwelcome desires.

If we indulge our mind, even for a little while, every day in chanting the holy names of Krishna—*Hare Krishna, Hare Krishna, Krishna Krishna, Hare Hare/ Hare Rama, Hare Rama, Rama Rama, Hare Hare*—and worship the Lord's deity form, study or hear from the Bhagavad Gita, Ramayana and Shrimad Bhagavatam and regularly associate with saintly people, we will gradually develop the much-needed inner strength, clarity of thought and sharp intellect, which will help us to not give in to our desires. This will reduce or eliminate our useless hankerings and lamentations.

Crave What Uplifts You

We have also often heard that desires are the root cause of suffering. But who would ever desire suffering? Everyone works for happiness but still, suffering often finds its way into our lives. Why is that? Because we may not desire suffering, but we desire things that may look like happiness, without knowing that they are a cause for our distress. This is owing to our ignorance.

What must one do then? Should we stop desiring or become desireless? That is simply not possible, even if we want to, because the soul, being a part and parcel of the unlimited Supreme Lord, is full of activity.

The problem is not with desires. It is the wrong kind of desires. Every desire we cultivate is like a seed sown that will give fruit in future. Thus, we must constantly watch the seeds we sow. We must purify our desires or desire the right kind of things. To achieve this, we need superior guidance, the guidance of a Guru.

It is just like a child, who doesn't know that putting his hand in fire will burn him; but the mother, who is more evolved in intelligence and experience, knows it and intervenes to prevent the child from touching fire.

Be Guided

Spiritually, we all are children; therefore, we need to be guided by a Guru. A Guru's job is not to cut down our desires but to simply help us cultivate the right kind of desires and help give up the wrong ones, so that we do not suffer in future. The Guru enters our lives, helps us align our desires in the right direction and saves us from getting hurt.

In essence, wherever we are today is the result of the desires cultivated in the past, and where we end up in the future will depend on the desires that we cultivate in the present. But to know which desires are bona fide, we need to seek the shelter of a bona fide Guru, thanks to whom our entire life will become a blissful experience.

11

Karma Yoga

The Art of All Work

The scriptures, that act like a guidebook for the human form of life, are written assuming we understand the ultimate goal of life: the realization of God. We might have immediate goals, but they should always be aligned with the ultimate goal. For our own benefit, we are expected to lead a life which will help us stay connected to God.

yajñārthāt karmaṇo 'nyatra
loko 'yaṁ karma-bandhanaḥ
tad-arthaṁ karma kaunteya
mukta-saṅgaḥ samācara

Bhagavad Gita (3.9)

> 'Work done as a sacrifice for Viṣṇu has to be performed; otherwise work causes bondage in this material world. Therefore, O son of Kuntī, perform your prescribed duties for His satisfaction, and in that way, you will always remain free from bondage.'

Good Karma Is Not Good Enough

Every action, whether good or bad, has an equal and opposite reaction. Only work done as service to the Lord, and keeping His pleasure as the goal, will lead to freedom from karmic reactions or suffering. If good, or pious acts of the world don't lead to liberation, where do we even begin speaking of sinful acts?

The soul may find a stairway to heaven, but as soon as the stock of piety is over, it stutters, falls down and comes back to this material world. It keeps going through the cycle of birth, old age, disease and death, over and over again. The soul remains bound to the laws of karma. And what is this bondage?

Imagine our hands and legs are tied with ropes. What happens then? We would want to eat something but won't be able to. We would want to move about but fail to. In essence, our movement will be restricted. We shall not be able to do what we desire.

Similarly, subtle as the ropes of karma are, they bind us in accordance with our actions. The laws of karma (action and reaction) are forced upon us, and we end up with no real independence. We are forced to go through old age, disease and death, even if we do not want to.

We would like to accomplish things in life, but we will not be able to, despite our best intentions. We will be misunderstood. Despite our best efforts, we will face major setbacks in life. The problems of life will not end, and we will end up getting the opposite of what we had set out to achieve.

Obedience = Freedom. Rebellion = Bondage.

Thus, our actions must please the Lord. We want to live free, but we must live by His laws. A citizen who lives by the laws of the state lives a free life, whereas a person who acts independent of the law gets punished.

Take the example of a soldier, who kills thousands of people at the border. But when he returns home, he is rewarded by the government. Then, one day, as he is moving around his city, he takes out his gun and shoots a person. However, this time, he gets punished by the same government. What is the difference? In the first instance, he was still killing people, that too a larger number, but it was sanctioned by the authority or the government; whereas in the second instance, he killed someone independently or whimsically.

Similarly, those who lead a life independent of God are punished by the laws of God, and upon those who endeavour to always serve and connect with Him, karma ceases to act.

Don't Renounce—Rewire

Humans are expected to live under certain regulations and in a certain way. Enjoyment is not forbidden, but it must be had with proper conduct. Activities may still remain the same, but how and for whose pleasure we act changes.

For long, we have been living a life centred around our own selfish pleasures, but now, we must resolve to engage in activities for God's pleasure as well. Live a life of connection, not rejection. That does not mean we give up our home, family or occupation. We simply need to add God (Krishna) to these activities.

But how?

It's no problem to own a large, palatial house, but we must also create a nice space for the Lord in it; a little temple where the entire family comes together to serve Him.

If we enjoy earning money, no problem, but we must use a portion of this money to serve Krishna, by serving His deity at home, making pretty arrangements for His service when celebrating festivals, offering nice food to Him, organizing satsangs or devotional events at home where His glories and names can be recited from the scriptures and supporting activities at a temple where the Lord is worshipped with utmost care, love and devotion.

If we enjoy eating good food, let us offer it to God first. This is how the food we consume becomes sanctified. If someone thinks: *In my house, the situation is not favourable as all family members are not on the same page, and therefore I cannot offer the food cooked at home*—no problem, offer something little every day. It could be juice, fruits and nuts, milk or sweets.

Offer it to the Lord and distribute the food among your family members. At least some sanctified food must go inside our system every day. This is Karma Yoga, or the art of living in this world. If we can incorporate these activities into our routine, we shall surely be protected from material infections (lust, anger, greed, pride or envy) and lead a life that is happy, unaffected by the inevitable ups and downs of life.

We must live in a way that each and every act of ours helps us come closer to God, and the acts must be in line with the laws made by Him. All the achievements, resources and facilities in life are a big zero, for they can end any moment. They have no real value in the long run. How many zeros we own does not matter. Only when we add a one before these zeroes does each of them become valuable. God is that one in our lives.

If we simply add him to all our activities and make him a part of our family life, our businesses and earnings, our enjoyments and joy, each of these things become the cause of real happiness. In this way, we can be in this world, but not of this world.

God Doesn't Judge Your Job

Once, there lived a pure-hearted person, who, owing to his profession, sold meat. One day, he came across a beautiful black stone lying on the pathway leading to his shop. He picked it up and decided to use it as a weighing stone when selling meat.

He would place the quantity of meat he wanted to sell on one side of the weighing scale and the stone on the other. But the black stone was magical. When the person wanted to sell half a kg of meat, the stone would assume the weight of half a kg. Likewise, the stone turned its weight to 2 kg the moment the person wanted to sell 2 kg of meat. This way, the person did not have to keep using different weights.

Interestingly, the meat seller would keep singing the Lord's names as he engaged in his daily work. He was living through his days blissfully until one day, a Brahmana happened to pass by his shop. When the Brahmana's eyes fell upon the black stone, he was horrified. He instantly recognized that the black stone was no ordinary stone but a 'Shaligram', a form of Lord Viṣṇu.

He chastised the person for keeping the Lord in such a dirty place; not just keeping it but using the Lord to sell meat. The person felt extremely heartbroken and guilty at his ignorance and begged forgiveness from the Brahmana. The Brahmana took the shaligram home, installed Him on a throne and started worshipping Him with awe and reverence. In line with Vedic rites, he chanted appropriate hymns and performed other rituals to clean and purify the stone.

But after a few days, the Lord appeared in the Brahmana's dream and said, 'What have you done? Where have you brought me? I was much happier at that meat shop.'

The surprised Brahmana asked, 'Why would you go back to that sinful place?'

The Lord replied, 'He may be selling meat, but that is his profession because of his past karmas. But when doing his job, the person kept singing my names with a pure heart. I am not impressed with your worship of reverence. I do not even see the external circumstances. I am only conquered by pure devotion.'

The Brahmana had no choice but to take the Lord back to the meat seller, who was obviously delighted to have his God back.

As per his past karmas, the person was born in the family of meat sellers. He could not do much about it and had to engage in the same profession. But while doing his daily chores, he would chant Krishna's holy names.

Just like the meat seller's case, it hardly matters where we are in life or what we do, as long as we use our position to connect with the Lord by chanting His holy names and listening to narrations about Him. In doing so, we will please the Lord and be blessed with good fortune.

12

Rituals

The Scientific Understanding

In today's fast-paced world, a common statement we hear is: 'I'm not very ritualistic.' It's often said with a sense of pride, as if distancing oneself from rituals equates to being progressive or rational. But have we ever paused to ask: what does 'being ritualistic' really mean?

I'm Not Ritualistic—Or Am I?

At its core, every aspect of life is shaped by rituals. From morning routines to fitness regimens, from national anthems to birthday celebrations—rituals are everywhere. They provide structure, meaning and continuity. The question is not whether we follow rituals, but *which* ones we choose to embrace.

The real problem arises when rituals become mechanical, devoid of understanding or connection. Spiritual practices, when done with awareness, are not empty traditions but powerful tools for inner transformation. True wisdom lies not in rejecting rituals altogether but in engaging with them consciously—in choosing those that uplift the mind and soul.

Cosmic Collaboration: Why Krishna Created Rituals

Lord Krishna Himself has put the rituals in place as stated in the Bhagavad Gita (3.10-11):

saha-yajñāḥ prajāḥ sṛṣṭvā
purovāca prajāpatiḥ
anena prasaviṣyadhvam
eṣa vo 'stv iṣṭa-kāma-dhuk

'In the beginning of creation, the Lord of all creatures sent forth generations of men and demigods, along with yajnas (rituals) for Viṣṇu.
, and blessed them by saying, "Be thou happy by this yajna because its practice will bestow upon you everything desirable for living happily and achieving liberation."'

devān bhāvayatānena
te devā bhāvayantu vaḥ

parasparaṁ bhāvayantaḥ
śreyaḥ param avāpsyatha

'The demigods, being pleased by sacrifices, will also please you, and thus, by cooperation between men and demigods, prosperity will reign for all.'

We have unlimited desires but do not have the power to fulfil them all on our own. Even basic survival in this world is impossible without the help of the higher, universal powers. In order to live, we need heat, oxygen, water and rain, just to count a few.

Krishna, out of kindness, created a community of celestial Gods, who are in charge of universal affairs and various necessities of human society. These celestial Gods, sometimes also addressed as 'demigods', are blessed with the powers of God to run the universe. They are like different individuals with different roles in an organization, managing various departments, empowered, also, to fulfil the material desires of living entities.

Krishna could do so Himself, but He does not deal with anything that is material. Even though material desires are not healthy, Krishna, like a loving father, facilitates their fulfilment. But He does so in a way that while having our material desires fulfilled, we are also making some spiritual advancement. Thus, a wonderful arrangement is made. The celestial Gods are given the power to fulfil our desires, and the human beings can take advantage of these powers by engaging in the prescribed rituals.

From Desire to Devotion: The Hidden Power of Rituals

So, rituals are the means to connect with and please these higher beings and God, who in turn bestow us with all things necessary to live a life. Since these rituals are coming from the Lord and He is the ultimate beneficiary of all our offerings, anyone who engages in them (with proper conduct) also has his consciousness purified.

Thus, Krishna creates this system of rituals where people who are not interested in Him, but only interested in fulfilling their material desires, can turn to these rituals for help, and in this way, indirectly get connected to Him because eventually all these rituals come from Him so that everyone can be happy and stay connected. When these people engage in His rituals, two things happen:

1. **Purification:** An individual has to engage in some kind of spiritual discipline, like fasting; he has to engage in some form of worship and control his senses; he must travel to holy places. When a person conducts all these activities, even with a goal to fulfil material desires, these rituals have the power to purify his consciousness from material contamination.

2. **Evolution:** A person gets to hear about the higher subject matter: that life is not just centred around, 'I, me and mine, or eating, sleeping, mating and defending.' He gets to understand the real goal of life, and this way, a person gains spiritual knowledge, getting purified at heart. The rituals eventually help him to rise to the realms of Karma Yoga.

At this level, a person starts thinking: all my life, I have lived simply trying to satisfy my own needs. Now, let me try to do something for God, too. Thus, a person's spiritual journey begins.

Hence, the ultimate purpose of performing rituals is to help the soul that is not directly interested in God to connect with Him indirectly and gradually make spiritual advancement.

Eventually, he comes to understand that the goal of life is to serve God; see everything and do everything keeping Him in mind. This is the real success in life. A life that is exemplary and can inspire countless people to stop living like animals and start living like real human beings and create a civilization based on spiritual culture.

Expression of Gratitude

In addition, rituals are also a way of expressing our gratitude to God. Being grateful is a sign of a cultured human being and that way, being 'non-ritualistic' means being ungrateful. There is no sin bigger than lack of gratitude in life. So, when we engage in these rituals/worship on a regular basis, we are essentially saying 'thank you' to God and all his agents running the universe, for blessing us with various necessities of life. Rituals, in a sense, are also like the tax that we pay to the universal government for the supply of oxygen, water, rains, food grains and other facilities we enjoy. If we simply keep receiving the supply and do not pay the bill, we will be considered thieves.

Take our food for example. We cannot survive on nuts and bolts. We live on food grains and these, in turn, are dependent on the rains. The rains, just like the sun and the moon, are dependent on the pleasure of the celestial gods. If there is no sun, there will be no life. If there is no moon, there will be no juice in the vegetation. If there is no rain, we can't have food grains.

In essence, the purpose of introducing these rituals in our lives is to help us fulfil our material desires, but with a sense of gratitude and simultaneously, to help us evolve to a higher consciousness.

A Way to Connect to Happiness

No one is really interested in God. Everybody is just interested in getting his or her material desires fulfilled, but Krishna knows that a person like this will never be happy. If we continue to act on the material realms, we will never understand that the only source of true happiness is in the service of God. We only grow and have value as long as we are connected to Him.

People spend so much time, money and energy in beautifying their nails. However, the moment we clip them, they fall and lose all their charm and value. Have we ever come across a person who asks the attendant at a salon to pick up their clipped nails and pack them, so they may carry the nails home and keep them in their living room for everyone to see? The clipped nails stop growing as well. They grow and look beautiful as long as they are connected to the whole body, the source. The sparks in fire have light and heat as long as they're in touch with the flames. As soon as they're separated, they are lost into oblivion. A finger attached to the hand has value as long as it is connected, but when it is cut, it becomes useless.

Similarly, as long as we are connected to our source, Krishna, we have real value, and we will continue to grow internally as well as externally. The moment we disconnect, there's only one way to go and it is down the hill (degradation of the soul).

So, before dismissing rituals as outdated, perhaps we should ask: *Are we truly free from rituals, or have we simply replaced sacred ones with mundane ones?*

13

Food

We Are What We Eat

Your Food = Your Future

What we put on our plate doesn't just fill our stomachs—it shapes our minds, energy and even destiny. Food is more than fuel; it carries vibrations that influence our thoughts, emotions and consciousness. A diet of purity nurtures clarity, while indulgence in tamasic or rajasic foods can cloud the mind and stir restlessness. Maximum contamination of the body and the mind happens due to the food we eat. Nowadays, people seem to have lost any sense of order or control when it comes to food habits—they eat whatever they like, whenever they want to, just to satisfy their taste buds. Forget the sinful karma that they may be accumulating, people are not even concerned about their health, although every day, newer and newer data suggests how the kind of food we are addicted to is the root cause of major health issues.

The Gita's Food Code

Depending on the kind of food we eat, we develop corresponding qualities. The qualities—or the lack of those—we acquire in life depend directly on the food we eat. For example, if we eat food that is pure and sattvic (in sattva guna), such as fruits, vegetables, nuts or milk, our thoughts will be pure, and we will develop a greater sense of happiness that is freed of sin, aiding clarity of thought.

As stated in the Bhagavad Gita (17.8):

āyuḥ-sattva-balārogya-
sukha-prīti-vivardhanāḥ
rasyāḥ snigdhāḥ sthirā hṛdyā
āhārāḥ sāttvika-priyāḥ

'Foods that are sattvic, or dear to those in the mode of goodness (sattva guna), increase the duration of life, purify one's existence and give strength, health, happiness and satisfaction. Such foods are juicy, fatty, wholesome and pleasing to the heart.'

Further, it is said in Bhagavad Gita (17.9-10):

kaṭv-amla-lavaṇāty-uṣṇa-
tīkṣṇa-rūkṣa-vidāhinaḥ
āhārā rājasasyeṣṭā
duḥkha-śokāmaya-pradāḥ

yāta-yāmaṁ gata-rasaṁ
pūti paryuṣitaṁ ca yat
ucchiṣṭam api cāmedhyaṁ
bhojanaṁ tāmasa-priyam

'Foods rich in "rajo" guna, or mode of passion, that are too bitter, sour, salty, hot, pungent or dry and cause a burning sensation cause distress, misery and disease. And if we eat food that aids the mode of ignorance, such as food prepared more than three hours before eating, or food that is tasteless, decomposed and putrid, and food consisting of remnants and untouchable things, then we develop qualities detrimental to our mental, physical and spiritual growth.'

Lord Krishna says in the Bhagavad Gita (14.8):

tamas tv ajñāna-jaṁ viddhi
mohanaṁ sarva-dehinām
pramādālasya-nidrābhis
tan nibadhnāti bhārata

> 'O son of Bharata, know that the mode of ignorance or "tamo" guna, is the delusion of all embodied living entities. The results of this mode are madness, indolence and sleep, which bind the conditioned soul.'

The choice is ours, for what we eat is what we become. We develop the qualities associated with the energy that the food carries.

Eating Sin?

The devotees of the Lord or those interested in evolving their consciouness never eat food that is not offered to Krishna first. When we offer our food to the Lord, it becomes pure, or karma-free. Lord Krishna endorses this in the Bhagavad Gita (3.13):

yajña-śiṣṭāśinaḥ santo
mucyante sarva-kilbiṣaiḥ
bhuñjate te tv aghaṁ pāpā
ye pacanty ātma-kāraṇāt

> 'The devotees of the Lord are released from all kinds of sins because they eat food that is offered first for sacrifice. Others, who prepare food for personal sense enjoyment, verily eat only sin.'

The food is purified, and any amount of karma present in it—due to how it was acquired, and the consciousness it attained owing to the person who cooked it—is nullified.

Why Krishna Doesn't Need Our Food—But Still Wants It

However, the real motive behind offering our food to the Lord is not just to make it karma-free and protect our mental state, but to express our gratitude to the Lord for having blessed us with food on our plates. Everything comes from God, so how can a person, who is cultured or evolved to eat, anything that is not first offered to Him?

In our homes, it is disrespectful or rude to partake something without first offering it to the elders of the family. A person who cooks only for his own sense of gratification or enjoyment, without offering it to the Lord, is a thief and a sinful person.

And how can a person who is a thief achieve any peace in life?

Thus, we offer food to the Lord, not because He needs it, but because we need it. He has unlimited agents or energies to serve Him. As soon as He desires, something, rather everything, manifests. Shri Radharani cooks for Krishna every day, and Her specialty is that she never repeats any dish. Krishna gets something new to eat daily. So, who are we to truly offer anything to the Lord? But we must, for He is pleased by our gratitude.

Imagine a child, who borrows money from his mother, and goes to the market to buy her a rose. The mother must feel extremely happy. Similarly, even though everything belongs to Krishna, when we offer Him what we have received from Him in the first place, He is pleased, and His pleasure makes sure that our sinful karmas, which are at the root of all our problems in life, are destroyed, thus leading to a healthier and happier life.

Sometimes, people take pride in being vegetarians. Vegetarianism is important, but it alone will not free us from all sinful reactions. Vegetarianism alone won't purify us. It does minimize the amount of violence that happens these days through the meat industry, but the important point is, as mentioned in the verse quoted above—Bhagavad Gita (3.13)—even if the food is vegetarian, it still amounts to sin if one is not offering it to Krishna first.

We have to rise higher than vegetarianism alone. We must become more cultured and show gratitude to the actual hand that feeds us.

How to Offer Food to Krishna Step-by-Step

We should offer our food to the deities or pictures of the Lord at our homes, keeping the following things in mind:

In preparing food, cleanliness is the most important principle. Nothing impure should be offered to God.

Always wash your hands thoroughly before entering the kitchen, and while preparing the food, do not taste it, for you are cooking the meal not for yourself but for the pleasure of Krishna.

Once the food is prepared,

1. Arrange portions of the food on dinnerware reserved only for this purpose; no one but the Lord should eat from His dishes. Do not forget to keep drinking water on the plate.
2. Place Tulsi leaves on all food items; at least one on the plate if not on all items.
3. Keep the plate in front of the Lord. Close the room/ altar/ curtain, or cover the offering so it is not visible to anyone.
5. Offer the food with your own hands. The easiest way to offer the food is simply to pray, 'My dear Lord Krishna, please accept this food,' and to chant each of the following prayers three times while ringing a bell,

namo mahā-vadānyāya kṛṣṇa-prema-pradāya te
kṛṣṇāya kṛṣṇa-caitanya-nāmne gaura-tviṣe namaḥ

'O most munificent incarnation! You are Krishna Himself appearing as Sri Krishna Chaitanya Mahaprabhu. You have assumed the golden colour of Srimati Radharani, and You are widely distributing the pure love of Krishna. We offer our respectful obeisances unto You.'

namo brahmaṇya-devāya go-brāhmaṇa-hitāya ca
jagad-dhitāya kṛṣṇāya govindāya namo namaḥ

'I offer my respectful obeisances unto Lord Kṛṣṇa, who is the worshippable Deity for all Brāhmaṇas, the well-wisher of cows and Brāhmaṇas and the benefactor of the whole world. I offer my repeated obeisances to the Personality of Godhead, known as Kṛṣṇa and Govinda.'

After offering the food to the Lord, wait at least five minutes for the Lord to partake in the preparations. Then, take the plate and transfer the food to a serving plate, and wash Krishna's dinnerware. The food is now sanctified, or it has become prasad, which literally translates to 'mercy' from Krishna.

Now, we may eat the prasad. And as we eat, we should try to appreciate the spiritual value of the food. Because Krishna has accepted it, it is no different from Him, so by eating, we will be cleansed of our sins. Such food is the perfect vaccination for mental and physical impurities.

14

A True Leader

Echoes of Our Actions

What if every word we spoke echoed in the lives of hundreds? What if every choice we made quietly shaped someone else's future?

Whether we realize it or not—we're already leaders. On social media, in our friend circles, in our families—someone is watching us, learning from us, imitating us.

In a world obsessed with going viral, we've forgotten that influence is not about popularity—it's about responsibility.

Leadership is not a crown to wear; it's a burden to carry with integrity. And when mishandled, it doesn't just break our image—it breaks lives.

That's why Krishna, the original life coach, declares in the Bhagavad Gita(3.21) that our actions set the bar for society.

yad yad ācarati śreṣṭhas
tat tad evetaro janaḥ
sa yat pramāṇaṁ kurute
lokas tad anuvartate

'Whatever action a great man performs, common men follow. And whatever standards he sets by exemplary acts, all the world pursues.'

We don't just live for ourselves—we lead by example, whether we like it or not.

A Leader's Karma Echoes Further

If the leader is good, the citizens or followers will automatically be good. It is the leader who is responsible for the happiness and distress of his followers. If he is sinful, the citizens suffer the reactions, too, and if he is pious, the followers are guaranteed a happy life. Thus, the greatest service we can do to our loved ones, and to society in general, is to set an example by leading a life that is sattvic, pure, sinless and based on religious (dharmic) principles or codes of conduct given by God for humanity—because whatever we do will impact those around us too.

Silent Followers, Loud Consequences

No matter who we are, we are bound to have some influence on the people we are connected to. Even if we are not inspiring millions, we are surely inspiring a few. People who look up to us will do what they see us doing. Thus, for anyone who is in a position to influence, or is a leader, it becomes his sacred duty to have good conduct and set the right example for others to follow.

Let us shed more light on this with a few examples. Parents, a king, a Guru or a leader, all have been given the same powers to impact the life of others. Parents have the maximum influence on their children. More than what the parents tell the children to do, they will do what they see the parents doing. If they see the parents respecting each other, respecting the elders of the family and following a disciplined lifestyle, the children will do the same. But if the parents are seen doing the opposite, the children will develop a similar character or mindset in life.

The Divine Clause

A king or a leader, if not of a good character, will motivate the followers to be characterless. One sixth of the karma, good or bad, of followers is shared by the king or the leader. This universal law, as per the dharma shastras, has been created to keep in check the people in a position to influence. When a person has been bestowed with the role of a leader, a lot more is expected of him in return, too. So, when the leader sets a good example of being selfless, sinless, pure or compassionate, the followers are inspired to do the same. As a result, he will share one-sixth of their good karma. However, if he behaves immorally and irresponsibly, the followers will engage similarly and, in addition to the reactions to his own bad karmas, one-sixth of his followers' bad karmas will also get added to his account. As a result, his suffering will be greater.

This provision has been made by God just so that people do not take their leadership or influential positions cheaply. Thus, if we have been blessed with a position of power, we must remember that it's a great responsibility and opportunity to serve, not to exploit or simply enjoy ourselves.

True Welfare: Body and Soul

A real leader should not be interested simply in the material advancement of his followers. The hallmark quality of a great leader is to make sure that his followers or subjects are not just advancing materially, but spiritually, too.

As the Shrimad Bhagavatam (5.5.18) states:

gurur na sa syāt sva-jano na sa syāt
pitā na sa syāj jananī na sā syāt
daivaṁ na tat syān na patiś ca sa syān
na mocayed yaḥ samupeta-mṛtyum

'One who cannot deliver his dependents from the path of repeated birth and death (by providing a

> strong spiritual foundation) should never become a spiritual master, a father, a husband, a mother or a worshippable demigod.'

At the same time, we should not be simply telling others to follow a God-conscious life. Instead, we must set an example of the same if we are to be accepted as true leaders. We must show others how we do not have to give up anything to make spiritual advancement. We must show people how, while executing our worldly duties, we can also attain spiritual perfection by simultaneously dedicating a portion of our time, energy and resources to God-centred activities.

Leading by Example

For example, we had kings such as Janak or Yudhishthir in the past, who were great rulers, had huge families, were busy expanding their kingdoms and, at the same time, were also great devotees of the Lord. They would act in a way that their followers would feel inspired to not just be morally right but also lead a life of devotion to God.

The kings would build temples and organize festivals centred around God. The citizens would feel extremely inspired to see the kings personally serve the Lord and engage in distributing spiritual food. The citizens would see the kings regularly invite saintly people into his courtroom and recite from the scriptures the beautiful narrations from the life of the Supreme Lord Hari. This would send a message across to the citizens that these activities were just as important as living a worldly life.

Similarly, we all are leaders in our own little kingdoms, and have influence over people. It could just be our family members, children, people working under us in our organizations and so on. It is our great responsibility to make sure that all those who look up to us are provided with a very strong spiritual foundation.

In essence, a leader must be a true servant of his followers by being exemplary in his words and actions that inspire others to walk the correct moral and spiritual path, so that they do not suffer in the future.

Yes, he must take care of their needs on the bodily platform, but the needs on the spiritual platform must also be looked after. The body is temporary, but the soul is eternal, and only when both these needs are taken care of properly, does it become a complete welfare system—help rendered to the body and help rendered to the soul.

15

The Avatars

Have you ever looked at the world and thought: *This is chaos. Who's in charge here?*

Corruption becomes culture. Truth becomes relative. And virtue? It's mocked, sidelined or forgotten. No matter how many laws we pass or leaders we elect, things still fall apart. Why? Because we—the supposed caretakers of Earth—come with four built-in flaws: Our senses are limited, we make mistakes, we cheat and we often live in illusion.

If humans are flawed by design, who sets things right when the whole system breaks down?

That's when HE comes.

Not as a tyrant or a hidden force—but as **an Avatar,** who doesn't just preach but lives the example. Time and again, Krishna descends—not because He *has* to, but because He *chooses* to.

As He Himself states in the Bhagavad Gita (4.7–8):

yadā yadā hi dharmasya
glānir bhavati bhārata
abhyutthānam adharmasya
tadātmānaṁ sṛjāmy aham

'Whenever and wherever there is a decline in religious practice, O descendant of Bharata, and a predominant rise of irreligion—at that time I descend Myself.'

To be precise, He apparently incarnates to fulfil three essential purposes as stated in Bhagavad Gita (4.8):

paritrāṇāya sādhūnāṁ
vināśāya ca duṣkṛtām
dharma-saṁsthāpanārthāya
sambhavāmi yuge yuge

'(1) To deliver the pious, (2) to annihilate miscreants, as well as (3) to re-establish the principles of religion, I Myself appear, millennium after millennium.'

To rescue the good. To crush evil. To restore balance. Like resetting a corrupted system from the inside out.

This chapter reveals why the world needs divine intervention, how these avatars aren't mythology but the greatest displays of compassion, and why even today, their grace is our only hope.

Because when humanity forgets how to live . . . **God comes to show us how.**

The Confidential Reason

However, Krishna, the God, the all-powerful, should be able to accomplish these tasks while sitting in His abode in the spiritual world through His various energies, right? Why then does He personally come down to this messy world?

Well, the answer can be found in the following episode:

> *One day, a king, curious about the nature of divine love, asked his wise minister, 'Why does your God behave so strangely? Doesn't your Lord Krishna have any servants? Each time a devotee calls for help, the Lord runs Himself. Surely, He can employ others to do such work?'*
>
> *The minister, with his sharp wit, decided to teach the king a valuable lesson. Knowing how much the king loved his grandson, he devised a plan. He asked a statue maker to create a lifelike dummy of the grandson and dress it in the same clothes as the young prince. He then instructed the guardian of the prince to carry the dummy to a lake and wait for his signal.*

After some time, he brought the king to the lake. At his signal, the guardian dropped the dummy into the lake. As soon as the king saw what he believed was his grandson being thrown into the water, he immediately jumped into the cold lake to rescue him. He swam as fast as he could and pulled the dummy out of the water, only to realize it was just a wax doll.

The minister then remarked, 'Your majesty, why did you jump into the lake yourself to rescue the young prince when you have so many guards and servants at your service?'

The king replied, 'Oh, I have hundreds of them, but my grandson is precious to me, so I couldn't stop myself. I could not wait.'

The minister smiled and said, 'Now you see, your majesty, that's why Lord Krishna, who loves each of His devotees dearly, comes to help them.'

The king, understanding the profound lesson, smiled and agreed with the minister.

Thus, the real reason why the Lord descends is to please and protect His devotees.

The Heart of Krishna

To Him, His devotees matter the most. They are His heart as He Himself declares in the Shrimad Bhagavatam (9.4.68):

sādhavo hṛdayaṁ mahyaṁ
sādhūnāṁ hṛdayaṁ tv aham
mad-anyat te na jānanti
nāhaṁ tebhyo manāg api

'The pure devotee is always within the core of My heart, and I am always in the heart of the pure devotee. My devotees do not know anything else but Me, and I do not know anyone else but them.'

And when the Lord comes, the killing of demons and re-establishment of dharma happen on their own. Lord Narasimhadeva (the fourth avatar of the Supreme Lord Krishna) did not appear to kill Hiranyakashipu. The demon was oppressing everyone in the three worlds, but when the celestial Gods approached Lord Viṣṇu (in charge of upholding peace in the universe), Lord Viṣṇu told them that as and when Hiranyakashipu troubles His dear devotee Prahalad, He would incarnate to kill him.

It is clear from this statement that the Lord does not interfere in the regular happenings of the material creation. He gets involved whenever His devotees need Him and for them, He is willing to break old rules and make new ones, which He usually does not do.

Types of Avatars

Most people simply know about the ten principal incarnations only, popularly known as the

'Dashavatars'. In reality, there are countless avatars, categorized as follows:

1. *Purusha avatars*
2. *Lila avatars*
3. *Guna avatars*
4. *Manvantara avatars*
5. *Yuga avatars*
6. *Shaktyavesha avatars*

1. Purusha avatars:

Krishna first incarnates as the three Purusha avatars, namely:

a. Karanodakashayi Viṣṇu: 'The Lord who is lying on the causal ocean and creates all countless material universes.'
b. Garbhodakashayi Viṣṇu: 'The Lord who is lying on the ocean within each of the universes and gives birth to Lord Brahma on a lotus sprouting from His navel, again in each universe.'
c. Kshirodakashayi Viṣṇu: 'The Lord who is lying on the ocean of milk within each universe and is in charge of the maintenance of that particular universe. Whenever there is some major disturbance, He intervenes.'

Since there are countless universes, there are countless Garbhodakashayi and Kshirodakashayi Lord Viṣṇus.

The duty of Garbhodakashayi Viṣṇu is to create Lord Brahma, who then does the secondary creation within the universe. Lord Kshirodakashayi Viṣṇu is in charge of sustaining the universe and all the avatars come through Him.

2. Lila avatars:

Following is the list of the Lila avatars (pastime incarnations) mentioned in the Shrimad Bhagavatam (Canto 1, Chapter 3):

Kumaras, Narada, Varaha, Matsya, Yajna, Nara-Narayana, Kardami, Dattatreya, Hayasirsa, Hamsa, Dhruvapriya or Prishnigarbha, Rishabha, Prthu, Narasimha, Kurma, Dhanvantari, Mohini, Vamana, Parasurama, Ramachandra, Vyasa, Balarama, Krishna, Buddha and Kalki.

3. Guna avatars:

The whole world is under the influence of the three gunas or qualities:

1. Sattva guna, or the mode of goodness, related to maintenance.
2. Rajo guna, or the mode of passion, related to creation.
3. Tamo guna, or the mode of ignorance, related to destruction.

The Lord manifests or incarnates in three forms to take charge of the same. Since Lord Brahma is responsible for creation, He manages the mode of passion. Lord Viṣṇu manages the mode of goodness, as maintenance is the most difficult part. And Lord Shiva is in charge of the mode of ignorance.

4. Manvantara avatars:

Brahma's one day, which is one thousand cycles of the four yugas (totalling to 4,32,00,00,000 earthly years), is divided into fourteen periods of the rule of Manus (fathers of mankind), known as Manvantaras. This means fourteen Manus come and go during one day of Lord Brahma. The incarnations during these Manvantaras are known as Manvantara avatars.

5. Yuga avatars:

In each of the four yugas, one particular avatar of the Lord descends with the specific purpose of giving the particular spiritual practice recommended for the respective yuga. He is known as the Yuga avatar.

In the Satya yuga, a white avatar appeared to Kardama Muni to establish meditation as the process for self-realization.

In the Treta yuga, a red avatar appeared to Brahma to establish fire sacrifice as the process for self-realization.

In the Dvapara yuga, a dark avatar (Krishna) appeared as the son of Devaki to establish temple worship as the process for self-realization.

In the Kali yuga, a yellow avatar appeared (Chaitanya Mahaprabhu) to establish the chanting of the holy names (*nama-sankirtana*) as the process for self-realization.

6. Shaktyavesha avatars:

Also known as the empowered incarnations, they are the lives invested by the Lord with His own spiritual potency to carry out a specific task. Sometimes, the Lord feels that He does not need to descend personally, thus He chooses a bunch of highly qualified individuals to carry out His will. There is no limit to the number of 'Shaktyavesha' incarnations. But some are mentioned in Vedic literature as examples:

1. Sage Narada is empowered to spread devotional service.
2. Lord Brahma himself is empowered with the power to create.
3. King Prithu (mentioned in Shrimad Bhagavatam, Canto 4) is empowered with the power to maintain living beings.
4. Parashurama is empowered with the power to kill evil elements
5. Sage Veda Vyas is empowered to compile the Vedas.

6. The four Kumaras, the first-born sons of Lord Brahma are empowered to spread knowledge.

He Will Keep Coming

Thus, in a world that often feels like it's spiralling into chaos—where truth is twisted, goodness is mocked and confusion reigns—this truth shines like a beacon: God has not abandoned us. He never has. He keeps coming.

He comes not just in ancient times or in mythic pasts, but He comes when the world forgets Him—and even more so, when we forget ourselves. Whether as Rama, Krishna, Narasimha or Chaitanya Mahaprabhu, each manifestation of the Lord is a divine response to a world that has lost its way.

But His descent isn't just about slaying demons or restoring cosmic balance. It's far more intimate. He comes to awaken and attract our hearts, to remind us of our eternal identity and to extend His hand—personally—to lead us back home.

Even now, through His words in the Gita, His holy names and the lives of His pure devotees, Krishna continues to incarnate in spirit and presence, reaching out to those willing to listen.

He is not far away.

He's just one sincere call away.

16

Is God Partial?

Wait, is God playing favourites? Does He take sides? What would you say if someone accused God of being partial? The following story answers it beautifully.

Imagine a scenario where a father is sitting in the courtyard of his house and witnessing his two sons playing.

Suddenly, one of the sons runs up to him and jumps onto his lap.

The father excitedly extends his arms and lovingly makes him sit on his lap and showers him with affection. A person standing close by witnesses everything and feels a bit confused and surprised at the same time.

He approaches the father, who is busy playing with his son and speaking sweet words to him, and asks, 'Hey, what kind of behaviour is this? You are supposed to be equal to all your children. You are just busy being so kind to this one, but what about the other one? He also deserves your love. Why this partiality?'

The father smiles and explains, 'Look, for me, both my children are equal. This one ran up to me seeking my attention and affection and being a loving father, I reciprocated his intention. The second one is busy playing right now and as and when he decides to approach me, he will also get the same attention. So, it is not about my being partial, but about what the children want. I am equally available to both.'

This simple moment unpacks a profound truth taught in the Bhagavad Gita (4.11): God is equal to all—but He reciprocates with the ones who approach Him.

ye yathā māṁ prapadyante
tāṁs tathaiva bhajāmy aham
mama vartmānuvartante
manuṣyāḥ pārtha sarvaśaḥ

'As all surrender unto Me, I reward them accordingly. Everyone follows My path in all respects, O son of Pṛthā.'

'You move first, He moves closer.'

He's Equally Available to All—but Especially Close to Some

God is equally available to all, while some people are close to Him and some are far away; some have faith in

Him and some remain faithless. Everything is purely the result of the individual's desires and choices. For those who want to get close to Him, He creates favourable situations in their lives, so that they can know Him and get to Him. As he says in Bhagavad Gita (8.29):

> *samo 'haṁ sarva-bhūteṣu*
> *na me dveṣyo 'sti na priyaḥ*
> *ye bhajanti tu māṁ bhaktyā*
> *mayi te teṣu cāpy aham*

> 'I envy no one, nor am I partial to anyone. I am equal to all. But whoever renders service unto Me in devotion is a friend, is in Me, and I am also a friend to him.'

Further, He says in Bhagavad Gita (10.10):

> *teṣāṁ satata-yuktānāṁ*
> *bhajatāṁ prīti-pūrvakam*
> *dadāmi buddhi-yogaṁ taṁ*
> *yena mām upayānti te*

> 'To those who are constantly devoted to serving Me with love, I give the understanding by which they can come to Me.'

Born Lost? Or Just Repeating Old Choices?

Those who do not want Him, render Him to create situations in their lives so that they will have no access to anything related to Him. And eventually, when a person keeps cultivating such an attitude, life after life, he is given birth in some godforsaken places or is born as a diehard atheist, paving the way for further degradation of the soul. This is the reason why some people are born in places or families where spiritual culture is non-existent, and atheism is the main religion.

When Krishna appeared five thousand years ago, He personally demonstrated this principle. With those who wanted Him (take the Pandavas, for example), He gave His association and protected them from innumerable calamities; those who did not (say, Duryodhana), could not even understand that He was God. Eventually, they were all destroyed. Thus, every choice we make either brings us closer to Him or takes us away.

Every Yes to God Opens a New Door

Suppose a criminal has been imprisoned. The government sends him food, but he refuses. The government sends medicines, but he refuses. The government sends a counsellor, but he refuses. What will the result be? The government will stop sending anything anymore, because the person has shown, by choosing to refuse every time, that he does not want these things. Similarly, whatever the past might be, every human being does get opportunities to reconnect with our source (Krishna, the Supreme Lord). These opportunities come in the form of invitations to attend gatherings with devotees, to hear and chant the Lords's message, name and His glories, to visit a temple or to contribute towards His service with our money or resources or study the scriptures. Every time we say a yes or a no to these invites, we are getting closer or farther from the Lord.

If we respond positively, the Lord, as an expression of His supreme favour and kindness, will give more such opportunities. However, every time we respond negatively, either due to lack of interest or prioritizing something else, we are sending a signal to the Lord that we do not want His grace.

As a result, a point comes in our existence where we will have no access to Him. We might get degraded to a lower species of life in our next birth, or if we are born as human beings, we might be born in places where knowledge about God is totally non-existent. Thus, we end up creating our own misfortune.

So, is God partial? Not at all. He is simply personal.

He mirrors our desire—if we take one step towards Him, He runs a hundred steps towards us.

Every prayer, every effort, every tear matters to Him.

But if we turn away, He lovingly waits, never forcing, only inviting.

The distance between us and God is not measured in miles, but in intentions.

So, when the next opportunity knocks, don't delay—run into His arms like the child on the father's lap.

17

One God or Many Gods?

If Krishna is the Supreme Lord—as declared in the Bhagavad Gita—then why do we see people worshiping so many other deities like Ganesha, Indra, Shiva or Surya?

The answer lies in what people are looking for.

What Are We Really Seeking?

Imagine walking into a shopping mall. One person walks into a grocery store to buy salt. Another heads straight to the electronics showroom for a new phone. Someone else goes to the food court. The choice depends on the goal.

In the same way, different people approach different deities based on what they desire in life. The celestial gods, often called demigods, are powerful beings who manage various functions of the universe on Krishna's behalf. They are like ministers in a government—working under the authority of the Supreme.

So, when someone desires wealth, success, health, rain or removal of obstacles, they may naturally turn to those empowered to provide such benefits—like Lakshmi, Indra or Ganesha. This isn't wrong—but it reflects a limited understanding of life's true purpose.

Krishna explains this clearly in the *Bhagavad Gita* (7.20):

kāmais tais tair hṛta-jñānāḥ
prapadyante 'nya-devatāḥ
taṁ taṁ niyamam āsthāya
prakṛtyā niyatāḥ svayā

'Those whose intelligence is stolen by material desires surrender to other gods and follow various rules of worship according to their own natures.'

In simple terms, when material desires dominate the heart, one naturally seeks quick, worldly results, and thus turns to those who can provide them.

But the Gita doesn't condemn such worship. Instead, it redirects the sincere seeker: If you're tired of temporary solutions and want eternal peace, love and liberation—go to the source.

Krishna is not just another God—he is *the* God, the origin of all.

So the real question is not 'who do people worship?' The real question is, 'what do they want?'

Because our object of worship will always reflect our goal in life.

Misunderstandings That Keep People Away

Even if people know that the goal of life is liberation—or moksha, freedom—from suffering, by going back to our real home, the spiritual world, and engaging in the service of the Lord there, they are plagued by another type of ignorance, which is that all Gods are equal. Thus, they believe that we can worship anyone and get the same result.

In addition, some people are simply not aware due to lack of access to the appropriate knowledge. And if they get knowledge, their ego does not let them unlearn what they have learnt from their family, society and, worst of all, TV serials.

All of this combined leads to most people never developing the right approach, even if the priority is material enjoyment. If the agents can offer material necessities, then the one who has given them these powers can also most certainly do it and, in fact, on a much greater scale.

Approach Krishna Directly

As Krishna Himself says in the Bhagavad Gita (2.46);

yāvān artha uda-pāne
sarvataḥ samplutodake
tāvān sarveṣu vedeṣu
brāhmaṇasya vijānataḥ

'All purposes served by a small well can at once be served by a great reservoir of water. Similarly, all the purposes of the Vedas can be served to one who knows the purpose behind them.'

Krishna is like the big reservoir of water and the demigods are like the small wells. How much water can a well supply? Only a small amount. But how much water comes from a reservoir? More than any number of wells combined, for the wells draw water from the reservoir itself. In addition, we do not need to make an effort to go to each well. We can collect everything from one spot with less effort.

Similarly, there are thirty-three crore demigods, each in-charge of fulfilling a particular material desire or necessity. How many will we keep worshipping to cater to our countless desires? Do we even have the time and energy for it? The fact is that all the demigods derive their power from Krishna Himself. So why not simply approach one person who can cater to all our needs?

As stated in the Shrimad Bhagavatam (2.3.10):

akāmaḥ sarva-kāmo vā mokṣa-kāma udāra-dhīḥ
tīvreṇa bhakti-yogena yajeta puruṣaṁ param

'A person who has broader intelligence, whether he be full of all material desire, without any material desire or desiring liberation, must by all means worship the Supreme Lord, the Personality of Godhead.'

He Always Gives More

Krishna always gives more than what we desire and far more than what we deserve. Little Dhruva (Shrimad Bhagavatam Canto 4, Chapters 8-13), having been insulted by his stepmother, wanted a kingdom greater than his great-grandfather, Lord Brahma, a position occupied by no one till that time in the history of creation. With this aim in mind, he performed austerities and pleased Lord Viṣṇu. But when he saw the most attractive form of the Lord, he was completely satisfied and did not want anything material anymore. He just wanted to engage in the devotional service of the Lord.

But the Lord was aware of his initial desire, too. So, the Lord did not just grant him the position he wanted but also unlimited material enjoyment with unchanged senses along with a long life in this world. Thus, by the blessings of the Lord, he got the best of both the worlds, a clear lesson for all aspiring for some material benedictions as to how to get things done in the best way. We must approach a person who has got more: more wealth, more beauty, more power and more capacity to give. This is real intelligence.

The Real Intelligence

In addition, Lord Krishna (Bhagavad Gita 7.23) calls the worshippers of demigods 'less intelligent'.

antavat tu phalaṁ teṣāṁ
tad bhavaty alpa-medhasām
devān deva-yajo yānti
mad-bhaktā yānti mām api

'Men of small intelligence worship the demigods, and their fruits are limited and temporary. Those who worship the demigods go to the planets of the demigods, but My devotees ultimately reach My Supreme planet.'

Less intelligent isn't a belittling word. It is used just to help people follow the right path and receive the highest benefit. These people have the intelligence, which is why they are approaching some higher power, but the intelligence is less since they are not approaching the highest power with the same amount of effort. Less intelligent also because the demigods' positions are temporary and thus, the boons given by them are also temporary. Krishna is eternal and His benedictions are also eternal and stay with us life after life.

If we want to worship the demigods, we can do so by giving them due respect as per their positions in relation to Krishna but keeping in mind their limitations. But our heart should be given to all the attractive forms of Krishna who, when pleased with our sincere devotional service, not only gives what we want but much, much more than what we deserve.

Won't They Get Upset?

A question may arise: If we start giving priority to Krishna worship, will the demigods not get upset?

Well, we should not try to impose our own consciousness on them. They are great souls, who are most happy when we worship Krishna. They are not envious like the worldly-minded people. In fact, even they become happy when we serve Krishna, as is revealed in the episode from the life of a great poet Chandidas.

There were two brothers. One was named Chandidas, who worshipped the Goddess Chandi, a fierce form of the Goddess Durga. His brother, however, was a devotee of Lord Krishna. Chandidas was wealthy, because worshipping Goddess Durga often brought prosperity. He had a huge garden and a grand palace, whereas his brother had a small shaligram deity (a small, black, worshippable form of Krishna) but lacked any flowers to offer.

Every day, the Vaishnava brother would look longingly at Chandidas's beautiful garden and think, 'There are so many flowers here, yet I have none for my shaligram.'

One day, as he gazed at the garden, he mentally offered a flower from it to his Lord. The next day, Chandidas (unaware of his brother's offering) picked that very same flower and offered it to the Goddess Chandi. To his surprise, she appeared before him immediately and said, 'I am pleased with you, Chandidas. What blessing do you desire?'

Astonished, Chandidas inquired, 'How come you have appeared today, Goddess? I worship you every day, yet today you have suddenly come before me. Please tell me why.'

The Goddess replied, 'Today, you offered me a flower that had already been offered to Krishna, making it His sacred prasad. Seeing that flower pleased me, and that is why I have appeared.'

Chandidas was confused and asked, 'If Lord Hari (another name for Krishna) is superior to you, why did you never ask me to worship the shaligram instead of you?'

The Goddess replied, 'You never asked me who was Supreme. Had you asked, I would have told you. I know who is supreme—Krishna is the Supreme Lord, and the shaligram is His worshippable form, not me. But since you were sincerely worshipping me, I allowed it, hoping that one day you would learn and find the true object of worship.'

Hearing this, Chandidas was filled with remorse. He said, 'I am truly sorry for wasting my life in ignorance. Please forgive me. From now on, I will worship Krishna.'

Goddess Chandi smiled and said, 'There is nothing to forgive. I am happy for you. Go and worship the Supreme Lord of the world.'

Filled with repentance, Chandidas composed many songs expressing his devotion for and realization of Lord Krishna and His beautiful pastimes with the Gopis of Vrindavan.

The One They All Point To

Thus, we understand that the celestial gods—respected and revered—are not competitors to Krishna, but His devoted servants. They fulfil material desires because that is their role, but their hearts are most pleased when someone begins to seek the root of all divinity—Krishna Himself.

Worship driven by desire is transactional. But worship born of devotion is transformational.

Even if our heart is currently attached to other deities, let our worship be selfless, respectful and done with openness. Because if we are sincere, they will guide us—not away from Krishna, but towards Him.

In the end, if we follow the path as above, all roads of truth converge at the same destination.

And the destination is not a concept. It's a person, Krishna—who is not just the giver of gifts, but the giver of Himself.

That's the highest benediction. And the purpose of all worship.

18

The Caste System

A common misconception is that the Bhagavad Gita promotes the caste system. However, this idea arises from misunderstanding the scripture, often by those who have never studied it seriously or have approached it without proper guidance.

Sacred knowledge cannot be grasped with a clouded and biased intellect. Just as we need a qualified teacher to master any material subject, the same applies to spiritual wisdom. The Gita itself emphasizes the importance of learning from a bona fide Guru, one who has deeply realized the truth through the teachings of their own Guru in an unbroken disciplic succession. Without this, misunderstandings are inevitable.

Misunderstood Wisdom

Krishna does not use the word 'caste' anywhere. Rather, He talks about a wonderful and hope-giving system, called the 'Varnashrama' system.

He mentions in the Bhagavad Gita (4.12):

cātur-varṇyaṁ mayā sṛṣṭaṁ
guṇa-karma-vibhāgaśaḥ
tasya kartāram api māṁ
viddhy akartāram avyayam

'According to the three modes of material nature and the work associated with them, the four divisions of human society are created by Me. And although I am the creator of this system, you should know that I am yet the non-doer, being unchangeable.'

As per the system, the society is divided into four social and four spiritual divisions as follows:

1. Social divisions
    - Brahmana
    - Kshatriya
    - Vaishya
    - Shudra

2. Spiritual divisions
    - Brahmachari

- Grihastha
- Vanaprastha
- Sanyas

As clearly understood from the verse, these divisions are not made on the basis of birth (as often misunderstood) but as per a person's qualities and activities. Thus, it is not a system of discrimination, but that of aligning the society's energies in the right direction, so that while executing their worldly duties, people can also make spiritual advancement and perfect their human lives.

Roles with a Purpose: Order, Not Division

A person is either born into a Brahmana, Kshatriya, Vaishya or Shudra family as per his own karma, and thus he comes with his own strengths and weaknesses. But after being born, how can a person know what he is supposed to do?

Imagine an organization with a hundred employees, but none of the employees have their roles defined. One day, they enter the office and do not know what to do. So, they start engaging in whatever comes to their mind because they feel they must do something, since they are part of an organization now. As a result, there is complete chaos and there is no productivity in the organization.

But when their roles get defined as per their qualifications—such as HR head, CFO, CEO, chairman, receptionist, peon and so on—everybody gets engaged in the correct manner, leading to their and the organization's success. They are able to make the best use of their time and energy rather than working whimsically with no or minimal result.

Krishna's Kindness

All human beings are born into this world as per their past karmas with a certain mindset. Krishna being the Supreme Lord knows what kind of work would suit a particular soul as per his nature to help him evolve spiritually. Therefore, He defines their roles by creating this system, called the Varnashrama system, thereby giving them birth in respective families and, in doing so, defining the duties of each of these four divisions.

These duties are designed on the basis of religious principles, so that in trying to fulfil their material necessities, one will also make spiritual advancement, which is what human life is meant for.

What is important to note is that the duties of the Brahmana are different from the duties of the other classes. But what is more important is that if each one sticks to their respective duties, each one has an equal opportunity to rise to the highest platform of self-realization or God-realization, in essence of perfecting one's human form of life and getting liberated. Thus, this system is an arrangement made by Krishna to give everybody an equal opportunity to evolve, irrespective of where they come from.

Imagine a teacher having a variety of students in a class. An intelligent student takes an exam and scores according to the quality of his answers. Another student tells the teacher that he has not studied the complete syllabus. The teacher tells him to not worry and write whatever he has learnt and whatever he knows. The third student comes and says he has not studied at all. The teacher asks him to write whatever he can. The fourth student comes and tells the teacher that he doesn't even know how to write. The teacher says, 'Do not worry. You just sit in the classroom.'

The teacher adds, 'If you all follow my instructions, I will make sure all of you clear the exam.' This is the supreme magnanimity of the teacher that even though all may not be qualified, they are still going to pass the exam.

This is exactly what the Varnashrama system is. No matter who we are, if we simply follow the instructions of the Supreme Teacher Krishna as given in the Bhagavad Gita, all of us have the opportunity to pass the final exam, which is to leave this world behind and go back to our original home, the spiritual world. This is considered to be the ultimate perfection of human life.

Every Role Matters

Life is not meant to expand our material liabilities but to wind them up. Thus, the Varnashrama system, understanding each individual's nature, weaknesses and strengths, engages everyone as per their propensities and helps them to lead a moral, spiritual life in line with the will of the Supreme Lord, thereby helping them prosper in this world and the next as well.

Society is the body of the Supreme Lord. Among the head, arms, belly and the legs of the Lord, can we say which part is most important? The Lord's lotus feet are as important as the head. In fact, the lotus feet are worshipped the most.

Take our own bodies, for instance. Even if one part goes missing, the body cannot function. Each body part has a unique function, absolutely essential for the smooth functioning of the body. Similarly, among social and spiritual divisions, all are equally important, and one cannot function without the other.

Thus, we should not fall prey to any misconceptions. Rather, we must use our God-given intelligence to focus on the actual goal of the system. Each one is unique, each one is important, and each has an equal opportunity to rise above one's lower nature to become a perfect human being.

To sum it all up, Krishna never says caste is determined by birth. He explains that one's role in society is defined by guna (qualities) and karma (activities), not lineage. It is ignorance—not the Gita—that has led to the rigid caste discrimination we see today.

19

Karma

Every day, we make choices. What to say, how to act, how to respond. But what if every choice was more than just a reaction—what if it was a seed?

In the Bhagavad Gita, Krishna reveals a truth that can change the way we see our lives: every action we take is karma. And with karma comes consequence.

Unlike animals that act mostly on instinct, human beings are blessed with a unique gift—free will. We can choose. And because we can choose, we are also held responsible. With greater freedom comes greater accountability.

Every Choice Plants a Seed

This is why our choices matter. With each decision, we shape our future—not just in this life, but in the next. Every action, no matter how small, carries weight. It either builds a path toward peace or lays the groundwork for future pain.

Still, life doesn't always feel so fair. We all face moments when we wonder, *'Why me?' 'What did I do to deserve this?'*

This is where karma becomes complex.

Krishna acknowledges this complexity in the Bhagavad Gita 4.17:

karmaṇo hy api boddhavyaṁ
boddhavyaṁ ca vikarmaṇaḥ
akarmaṇaś ca boddhavyaṁ
gahanā karmaṇo gatiḥ

'The intricacies of action are very hard to understand. Therefore, one should know properly what action is, what forbidden action is, and what inaction is.'

The Three Kinds of Karma

Krishna breaks down karma into three categories:

1. **Karma—*Right Action***
   Selfless acts that benefit others—like feeding the hungry, helping the sick and speaking truthfully. These actions uplift the soul and bring future happiness, prosperity and even a better next birth.

2. **Vikarma—*Wrong Action***
   Actions that harm others or violate moral and spiritual principles—such as lying, cheating, hurting or exploiting. These lead to suffering, both now and in the future, and pull the soul deeper into ignorance.

3. **Akarma—*Transcendental Action***
   Actions done not for reward or reputation, but as an offering to God. These are beyond good and bad. They free one from karma altogether and lead to spiritual liberation.

Understanding karma is not just philosophy—it's power. When we become conscious of how and why we act, we gain control over our destiny.

Good Isn't Good Enough

Just performing good deeds is not enough as it does not guarantee freedom from reactions to our sinful acts. Good karma does not nullify bad karma. Both will be dealt with separately. Only God-conscious activities cancel out reactions to the bad and even elevate us beyond the good. Thus, it is important to also engage in the devotional service of the Lord, beginning with chanting His names (*Hare Krishna, Hare Krishna, Krishna Krishna, Hare Hare/Hare*

Rama, Hare Rama, Rama Rama, Hare Hare), hearing His beautiful narrations, worshipping His deity form and contributing to His mission. These activities do not just give us the strength to deal with what we are going through but also protect us from future suffering by destroying the sinful reactions that are yet to come as a result of our bad choices, made knowingly or unknowingly.

But Who Decides?

Now, the most important point is: who decides what is good or bad and where can we find the proof of it? How do we know what is 'dharma' (real duty or action) and what is 'adharma' (forbidden or sinful, immoral action)?

In today's day and age, the general tendency is to do whatever makes one happy. Even a hog or dog is happy doing what it does. Even a terrorist is happy by killing others. So, this logic does not work. Another common idea: whatever everyone else or the majority does is considered to be good. Well, the majority doesn't decide what is good and what is bad. Right is right even if no one does it, and wrong is wrong even if everyone does it. Then, who decides?

Denial Does Not Save Anyone

Just as in a city, where the government decides the laws and the citizens are expected to follow the same to live peacefully, in the universe the Supreme Lord is the one who decides what is good and what is bad. Just as a citizen who breaks the law as per his choice will be punished, similarly, those who break God's laws must suffer.

For example, it is our duty to stop at the traffic signal when the light turns red. But if we think that we won't stop because our favourite colour is pink and we speed past the signal, we might think we did the right thing by following our heart. However, the law does not change for us, and we will be penalized for breaking it.

The Real Laws

The Shrimad Bhagavatam (6.3.19) says:

> *dharmaṁ tu sākṣād bhagavat-praṇītaṁ*

> 'Real religious principles are enacted by the Supreme Lord.'

And these laws made by God do not change with time. We might say that the times have changed and now these things don't hold true, but the truth is that the laws have not changed. And these laws are to be found in our law books: the scriptures, which are the words of God. Whatever the scriptures consider good is good, and whatever the scriptures say is bad is bad, because that is the word of God.

Our choices, thus, should be based on the scriptures and not on some popular opinion or latest trends on social media or even what makes us happy. If everyone does something that is sinful, everyone will suffer. The majority does not matter.

The Reaction Will Come

Karma is like a seed. When we sow a seed, it does not fructify immediately. Some do in two or three days, and some take years. Similarly, whenever we engage in any act, good or bad, its fruits may not be seen immediately—but they are bound to come in due course of time. Thus, those who think they can go on engaging in sinful habits (primarily meat eating, intoxication, illicit affairs and gambling) or can cause pain to others thinking they cannot do anything to retaliate, must remember these acts are like seeds sown. The reactions will certainly come, sooner or later, and will turn our world upside down.

And not just us, those near and dear to us, especially our children, will also have to share the consequences. This is the law of karma. We must not run after instant gratification. It may give us a thrill for the moment, but the reactions would have to be borne for an entire lifetime. The mills of God grind slowly, but they grind exceedingly fine.

As You Sow

Those who lead a pure, sattvic and sinless life based on religious principles will experience happiness and peace even if there is complete chaos all around. But those who lead a sinful, irreligious and immoral life will not be able to live a life free of anxiety, even if there is peace all around them.

Everyone is busy making choices to be happy, but we must remember that happiness, success, satisfaction, contentment, fame and prosperity in life are the result of a pious, sattvic, pure life, based on religious principles. Similarly, distress, failure, setbacks, disappointment, pain and suffering in life are the result of leading a whimsical, sinful, immoral and irreligious life.

A Useful Analogy

Now, imagine a weighing scale with two sides: A and B. Side A is the good side with a pious, sattvic and sinless life; side B is the bad side, with an irreligious, immoral and sinful life. Depending on which side is heavier, a particular situation, such as prosperity or pain, will manifest in our life. If side A is heavier, we will experience tranquility, peace and happiness, whereas if side B is heavier, we will experience the opposite in the form of pain and setbacks.

Thus, if we wish to have a better life, we must make better choices, in order to be rewarded with a prosperous life. As we sow, so shall we reap.

When life feels heavy—when stress, setbacks or sadness overwhelm us—the natural tendency is to feel helpless, anxious, or even hopeless. But the Bhagavad Gita gives us a different lens: understand karma and take responsibility.

Instead of asking, '*Why is this happening to me?*' ask, '*What can I do now to create a better future?*'

Karma is not punishment—it's correction. And the best part? It can be changed.

Shift the Weight

If things aren't going well, don't panic—shift the weight. Start loading the 'A-side':

- Do more good. Help others, speak kindly, live with integrity.
- Deepen your spiritual practices. Chant, pray, read the Gita, serve.
- As this side grows heavier, the scales of life begin to tip. Slowly but surely, favourable opportunities, peace of mind and inner strength begin to return. This is not magic—it's spiritual science.

But remember: right action must be rooted in right knowledge. Our choices should align with the scriptures and be guided by those who live by them—saintly people who walk the talk.

Make this your principle:

'Let my actions be scripture-based and spiritually guided.'

Live by that, and you'll never regret your decisions—even in the toughest times.

In the end, karma is not just about past actions—it's about the present power to choose. And when we choose rightly, life responds.

Let your karma work *for* you—not against you.

20

Gaining Knowledge

The Right Way

We live in a world flooded with information. With a few taps on our phone, we can learn how to cook, code, meditate or lose weight. There are books, videos, podcasts—and now even AI—to guide us. But despite all this, when we truly want to learn something deeply, what do we do?

We find a teacher. When we want to lose some weight, even though all the information to do so is available on the Internet, and so many books have been written about the same, we still look for guidance from a dietician.

All kinds of books are available in the market, the knowledge is accessible on the Internet and now, AI supplements this repository. Still, when we want our children to learn a particular subject, we send them to a school to learn from a teacher.

Whether it's hiring a fitness coach, enrolling our children in school or seeking a mentor in our career, we instinctively know that real understanding comes from guidance—not just from reading on our own.

But strangely, when it comes to spiritual life, many abandon this common sense.

People assume they can understand God, the soul or the mysteries of karma by simply browsing the internet or flipping through a scripture. But spiritual knowledge is not theoretical—it's transformational. It is no exception. The method remains the same. To learn the subject of spirituality and religion, we must approach a bona fide Guru.

Krishna confirms this timeless truth in the Bhagavad Gita (4.34):

> *tad viddhi praṇipātena*
> *paripraśnena sevayā*
> *upadekṣyanti te jñānaṁ*
> *jñāninas tattva-darśinaḥ*

> 'Approach a self-realized spiritual master with humility, sincere inquiry, and service. Such enlightened souls can impart knowledge because they have seen the truth.'

Just because we know the language, it doesn't mean we understand the subject. We could read hundreds of pages on music, but that won't make us a musician. In the same way, to truly realize spiritual truth, we need someone who has walked the path and seen the reality for themselves—a genuine Guru.

This chapter will help us understand why a spiritual teacher isn't optional—it's essential. And how approaching the right guide can change not only what we know, but who we become.

The path of spiritual realization is undoubtedly difficult. Therefore, the Lord advises us to approach a bona fide spiritual master in the line of disciplic succession, or Guru-Shishya *parampara*, coming down from the Lord Himself. No one can be a bona fide spiritual master without following the principle of disciplic succession. The Lord is the original spiritual master, and only a person in the disciplic succession can convey the message of the Lord in its true essence. No one can realize spirituality by manufacturing their own process, as is the way of some foolish pretenders.

The path of religion is directly enunciated by the Lord. Therefore, neither mental speculation nor dry arguments help lead one to the right path, nor can an independent study of books help one progress in spiritual life. One must approach a bona fide spiritual master to receive the knowledge. Such a spiritual master should be accepted in complete surrender, and one should serve the spiritual master like a menial servant, without false prestige. Pleasing the Guru is the only secret to advancement in spiritual life.

Inquiry and submission constitute the proper combination for spiritual understanding. And when we enquire, it must be done in a submissive, not in a challenging way. The person enquiring is always in a lower position, and knowledge is always imparted from a higher to a lower platform, not the other way around. Knowledge cannot even flow on an equal platform. As long as Arjuna continued to argue, considering Krishna to be his friend, Krishna did not impart any knowledge. Only when Arjuna surrendered and submitted to Krishna did He actually start speaking.

In the journey of spiritual life, information is not enough—transformation is the goal. And transformation doesn't happen through casual reading or passive browsing. It happens through humble inquiry, heartfelt service and the shelter of a genuine spiritual teacher.

Krishna makes it clear: without humility and service, even the most profound knowledge will fail to touch the heart. It may inflate the ego, but it won't purify the soul.

A true Guru doesn't just answer your questions—he watches how you ask them. He tests, guides, corrects and lifts you—not to control you, but to prepare you. When the disciple is sincere, the Guru gives not just knowledge, but realization.

In today's world, many are misled by self-declared teachers, instant gurus, and spiritual shortcuts. But the Bhagavad Gita calls us back to what is real: find a bona fide spiritual master—one who lives by the teachings, not just speaks them.

So here's your call to action: Approach a genuine Guru.

Be humble. Ask with sincerity. Serve with devotion.

Let the flame of spiritual knowledge be passed into your heart—not just your intellect.

Because when you find the right teacher—and become the right student—the path opens, the fog clears and Krishna Himself becomes your guide.

Don't walk this path alone. You will be lost.

Find your guide. Begin your transformation.

21

Mind Your Mind

A man was sitting under a tree when a snake bit him. He wondered what caused him the pain, and as he turned around, he saw a mouse. He concluded that a harmless rodent had bitten him, and didn't think much of it. A few days later, while he was sitting under the same tree, this time the mouse bit him. Again, he wondered and looked around to find a snake slithering by. He thought the snake must have bitten him and died of the shock.

A short story that teaches a pertinent lesson about how our mind works. It wasn't the snake or the mouse that caused the problem. It was his mind.

This simple story reveals a profound truth: our mind often creates its own version of reality. It convinces us of things that aren't true, blinds us to what actually is and leads us into confusion, causing bias and prejudices in our hearts. It is flickering and stubborn and can turn a perception into a reality.

Same Tool Can Save or Destroy

Imagine holding a knife. In the hands of a skilled surgeon, it becomes a tool for saving lives. But in the hands of a criminal, it turns into a weapon of destruction. The knife itself is neutral—its value depends on who wields it and how it is used.

Now, imagine our mind as that knife. It's sharp. It's powerful. And it can be used in two drastically different ways.

In the hands of a disciplined, spiritually trained individual, the mind becomes a surgeon's tool. It cuts through illusion, doubt and distraction. It brings clarity, peace, purpose and joy. It becomes your best friend—one that guides you towards higher truths and lasting fulfilment.

But in the hands of someone careless, untrained or ego-driven, that same mind becomes a dangerous weapon. It spirals into negative thinking, jealousy, pride, anxiety, lust and greed. It convinces you of false realities, magnifies fears, fuels unhealthy desires and ultimately leads to self-sabotage and suffering.

Even Heroes Struggle

Arjuna, one of the greatest warriors of all time, also acknowledged the difficulty of controlling the mind. In Bhagavad Gita (6.34) he confesses:

cañcalaṁ hi manaḥ kṛṣṇa
pramāthi balavad dṛḍham
tasyāhaṁ nigrahaṁ manye
vāyor iva su-duṣkaram

'The mind is restless, turbulent, obstinate and very strong, O Krishna, and to subdue it, I think, is more difficult than controlling the wind.'

These words weren't spoken by someone weak or untrained. They were spoken by Arjuna—one of the greatest warriors in history.

Arjuna wasn't just a fearless fighter. He was focused, disciplined, intelligent and deeply spiritual. He had been trained in warfare, logic, scripture and morality from childhood. He had faced death on the battlefield, resisted temptation and upheld dharma (righteousness) in some of the most complex situations.

And yet—even he confessed that controlling the mind felt harder than controlling the wind. Just pause and think about that.

The wind is wild, invisible, constantly shifting and impossible to grab or stop. And Arjuna, with all his inner strength, compares the mind to something even more uncontrollable.

So what does that say about the rest of us—living in the modern world, surrounded by distractions, overstimulation, social media, constant comparisons, temptations and endless noise?

It means one thing clearly: We cannot afford to take the mind lightly.

The Slippery Slope

The mind is like a restless child or an uncontrollable monkey, jumping from one thought to another, chasing pleasure and avoiding discomfort. It gravitates toward what is easy and pleasurable, often tempting us to take shortcuts, even when they are unethical, imprudent or self-destructive.

At first, the mind merely tests our moral boundaries, tempting us with small compromises. But once we give in, it pushes further and further, eroding our ethical foundation bit by bit. What once seemed unthinkable eventually becomes normal. The very things we once condemned, we may one day find ourselves justifying or even embracing.

Many who have fallen into addictions, deceit and moral corruption never intended to walk that path. It began with one small compromise—one moment of weakness. But the mind, like an insatiable force, kept pushing the boundaries until what was once unacceptable became second nature.

When children aren't parented properly, they are most likely to become miserable adults and make all those around them miserable, too. The same applies to our mind. It is by such pandering to the mind that some people end up as addicts.

Train or be Trapped

That's why training our mind is not just a casual choice to be adopted so that we become better, but a vital obligation that, if neglected, can have catastrophic consequences for us and those around us. Thus, it is very important to control the mind.

We can train the mind in the following ways:

Education: This education refers not so much to attending classes or doing courses, but for gaining a well-informed vision of reality from the scriptures. By regularly studying the wisdom in the Gita, we can get our mind to appreciate and remember what is truly meaningful and valuable. Though the mind may presently crave for one sensual thing after another, steady scriptural study will infuse it with the gravitas to analyse and realize the things that matter the most. And because the spirit lasts forever, it matters the most.

Association: Despite knowing what is really valuable, the mind can, by its illusions, create an alternative reality wherein whatever it impulsively fancies is seen as the most valuable. To get the mind out of such fantasies, we need to place ourselves with individuals who cherish and relish what is truly valuable.

Most empowering is the association of spiritualists. Seeing their taste for higher spiritual things, our mind will start rethinking its petty infatuations. Even if it doesn't give them up immediately, being in good association will repeatedly remind it that its default actions differ so radically from theirs. Such reminders will have two salutary effects: make the mind hesitate to act out its impulses indiscriminately and give it impetus to pursue more meaningful things.

Purification: Intellectual and social impetuses are most effective when the mind's tastes evolve from lower to higher. We can accelerate such change by focusing the mind on the all-pure supreme reality, Krishna. That contact will purge the mind of its many impurities that distort its tastes. The more it becomes purified, the more it will relish things connected with the all-attractive Krishna, thereby naturally gravitating towards Him. The best way to do so is chanting Krishna's holy names—*Hare Krishna, Hare Krishna, Krishna Krishna, Hare Hare/Hare Rama, Hare Rama, Rama Rama, Hare Hare.*

The mind is very sensitive to sound. In Sanskrit, it is known as '*mann*', and the most powerful weapon to control the mann is mantra: that which liberates the mann is called mantra.

When we chant the mantra consisting of God's names, the mind gets purified of its lower taste and begins to focus on what really matters.

Krishna's Way

For a person trying to evolve in values and especially advance in spiritual life, dealing with the mind is the main challenge. Krishna Himself, after acknowledging the power of the mind, gives a twofold method to control the mind:

1. Detachment from sense objects.
2. Feeding the mind with positive alternatives.

A spiritualist is like a car driver and a jockey. Initially, when learning to drive, the driver finds it difficult to steer the car on the road. Later, with practice, he learns better. Similarly, a spiritualist can bring the mind on the track of God-consciousness. An expert jockey controls the horse by not restraining the horse too much and also by not allowing it too much freedom. Similarly, a spiritualist regulates his horse-like mind by careful supervision and gradually, but surely, manages to make it the best friend.

Entirely Our Choice

Essentially, the mind doesn't ask for permission. It doesn't wait for logic. It simply runs—either towards elevation or destruction.

That's why Krishna warns in the Bhagavad Gita (6.6):

bandhur ātmātmanas tasya
yenātmaivātmanā jitaḥ
anātmanas tu śatrutve
vartetātmaiva śatru-vat

'For one who has conquered the mind, the mind is the best of friends. But for one who has failed to do so, the mind remains the greatest enemy.'

In other words, we either master our mind—or it masters us. There is no neutral ground.

This is not a motivational slogan—it's a spiritual truth. If we want peace, purpose, and progress in life, we must learn to take control of our inner world. The stakes are high, and the consequences of neglecting this responsibility ripple through every area of life—relationships, decisions, career and spiritual growth.

The mind is our most powerful asset, or our most dangerous liability.

If we fail to control our mind, it will pull us toward ignorance, distortion and suffering. But if we train it through discipline, wisdom and guidance, it will lead us toward truth, fulfilment and liberation.

The choice is ours: Who's holding the knife?

Will we allow the mind to control us and dictate our actions? Or will we rise above its restlessness, take control and seek truth with clarity and sincerity?

The path to true wisdom begins not with intellect alone, but with mastering the mind—just as Krishna instructs Arjuna on the battlefield of Kurukshetra.

22

The Real Yogi

Yoga has become a buzzword, and the number of people claiming to be yogis or yoga masters has been growing day by day. From social media influencers to fitness trainers, everyone seems to be doing it. Studios are filled, mats are sold by the millions and more people than ever are calling themselves yogis or yoga masters.

But amidst all the noise, one essential question often goes unasked: What exactly is yoga? And who is a true yogi?

Is yoga merely about bending the body, controlling the breath or calming the mind? Is a yogi someone who can perform complex postures or meditate in silence?

According to the timeless wisdom of the Bhagavad Gita, the answer goes much deeper.

Krishna's Definition

A true yogi has been defined by Krishna in the Bhagavad Gita (Chapter 6, verse 6.47):

> *yoginām api sarveṣāṁ*
> *mad-gatenāntar-ātmanā*
> *śraddhāvān bhajate yo māṁ*
> *sa me yukta-tamo mataḥ*

> 'And of all yogis, the one with great faith who always abides in Me, thinks of Me within himself and renders transcendental loving service to Me—he is the most intimately united with Me in yoga and is the highest of all. That is My opinion.'

According to the highest authority, the Supreme Lord Krishna, a real yogi is the one who is intimately connected to Him in loving devotional service and is always remembering Him. The Bhagavad Gita is known as Yoga Shastra. Yoga means to link or connect with the divine or the Supreme Lord. Unless the goal of yoga practice is not this connection, it is not yoga, but some sort of gymnastics.

The Eight Steps of Yoga

Yoga has eight stages, starting with dhāraṇā, dhyāna and ending with the eighth and the last stage, which is called samādhi.

Samādhi means complete absorption in the thoughts of the Lord, a stage where even for a moment, a person's mind does not waver from Krishna. This is the ultimate goal of performing yoga.

Nowadays, the yoga that is being performed is only based on two aspects: āsana, prāṇāyāma, and not with the goal of connecting with God. It is being performed so that we can have a healthy body and sense enjoyment.

Lord Krishna talks about the eightfold yoga system in the sixth chapter of the Bhagavad Gita. The first and foremost aspect of this yoga system is the control of the mind and the senses, to withdraw them from sense objects and learn to focus on only one object. When we are fully accomplished in the same, our focus ultimately remains on God with undivided attention. This is the culmination of the Ashtanga Yoga wherein, a person experiences unlimited happiness and realises that there is nothing higher than this and nothing more to be gained.

The Arduous Process

As described by Yogeshwar Krishna (the master of all mysticism) in the Bhagavad Gita (6.20-23):

yatroparamate cittaṁ
niruddhaṁ yoga-sevayā
yatra caivātmanātmānaṁ
paśyann ātmani tuṣyati

sukham ātyantikaṁ yat tad
buddhi-grāhyam atīndriyam
vetti yatra na caivāyaṁ
sthitaś calati tattvataḥ
yaṁ labdhvā cāparaṁ lābhaṁ
manyate nādhikaṁ tataḥ
yasmin sthito na duḥkhena
guruṇāpi vicālyate
taṁ vidyād duḥkha-saṁyoga-
viyogaṁ yoga-saṁjñitam

'In the stage of perfection called trance, or samādhi, one's mind is completely restrained from material mental activities by practice of yoga. This perfection is characterized by one's ability to see the Self by the pure mind and to relish and rejoice in the Self. In that joyous state, one is situated in boundless transcendental happiness, realized through transcendental senses. Established thus, one never departs from the truth, and upon gaining this he thinks there is no greater gain. Being situated in such a position, one is never shaken, even in the midst of the greatest difficulty. This indeed is actual freedom from all miseries arising from material contact.'

Connection Is the Key

If, in our yoga, there is no deepening of connection with God, then that is not yoga at all. Krishna asks Arjuna to be a yogi in all circumstances, which means that He is telling all of us through Arjuna to stay connected to Him because a disconnected life is abominable. We have value, and our life becomes worth living, only when we stay connected to our source, Shri Krishna, the Supreme Lord.

Take the example of nails. People spend so much time, energy and money in keeping their nails attractive, but as soon as those nails are cut, they lose all the attractive power and stop growing. Or Or for that matter the hair on our head that we spend so much time taking care of, dyeing in different colours and fashions—but as soon as they are cut, they become unattractive. In fact, if we touch chopped hair, by the ideal Vedic standards, we need to bathe.

Similarly, we are all parts and parcels of God, Shri Krishna, and the more we stay connected to Him, the more we grow and evolve. Else, we will be lost to the karmic cycle, life after life.

The Ways to Connect

And how do we stay connected to Him? The Shrimad Bhagavatam mentions nine different ways, beginning with hearing about Him from scriptures like the Bhagavad Gita and the Shrimad Bhagavatam, chanting His names (easiest and most powerful), remembering Him by worshipping His deity form and so on. We can follow all, or some or even one of these methods and spend some time every day reviving that connection with the Lord.

Thus, the real goal of yoga is not power, prestige or personal perfection—it is pure devotion. A true yogi is not one who seeks to become God, but one who seeks to serve God with love and humility.

Even health, strength and discipline gained through āsana, prāṇāyāma find their highest purpose when offered in the service of Krishna.

The measure of our yoga is not in how well we stretch, but in how deeply we surrender. When the motive shifts from self-centered goals to God-centered service, only then do we become true yogis.

23

One in Trillions

Most people never even attempt to seek truth. And among those who do, only a rare soul truly succeeds.

Krishna reveals this in Bhagavad Gita (7.3):

manuṣyāṇāṁ sahasreṣu
kaścid yatati siddhaye
yatatām api siddhānāṁ
kaścin māṁ vetti tattvataḥ

'Out of many thousands among men, one may endeavour for perfection, and of those who have achieved perfection, hardly one knows Me in truth.'

Look around. How many people actually care about understanding life's purpose? How many are lost in the endless cycle of school, career, entertainment, relationships and fleeting pleasures—without ever questioning the deeper meaning of our existence?

The world is full of billions of people chasing temporary achievements—money, status, pleasure. But how many strive for self-realization? How many genuinely seek to know God?

Krishna says, only a handful even attempt to walk this path, and among them, only a rare soul truly realizes the ultimate truth.

The Privilege of Being Human

The term *manuṣyā* refers to a human being, a life form unique in its capacity for spiritual realization. The universe teems with countless forms of life. As stated in the Padma Purana (Brahma Khanda, 2.27-28):

jalajā nava-lakṣāṇi
sthāvarā lakṣa-viṁśati
kṛmayo rudra-saṅkhyakāḥ
pakṣiṇāṁ daśa-lakṣaṇam
triṁśal-lakṣāṇi paśavaḥ
catur-lakṣāṇi mānuṣāḥ

'There are 9,00,000 species living in the water. There are also 20,00,000 non-moving entities such as trees and plants. There are 11,00,000 species of insects and reptiles and there are 10,00,000 species of birds. As far as animals are concerned there are

30,00,000 varieties and there are 4,00,000 human species.'

Within this vast spectrum of life, humans occupy a special position. There are 4,00,000 distinct forms of human life, each varying in colour, shape and appearance. This list of species does not simply refer to the world we know of but to the entire universe. This diversity is a reflection of the intricate design of creation. Yet, the human form stands apart, as it alone possesses the ability to understand the deeper truths of existence, including God.

In human society, a process exists through which one can realize God—this process is known as religion. Religion is not merely a set of rituals but a means of discovering our true relationship with God and understanding our duties toward Him. The ultimate goal of human life is to fulfil this mission of spiritual awakening.

When Lord Krishna speaks to Arjuna in the Bhagavad Gita, He doesn't start with vague ideas about being kind or doing good. He goes straight to the most important question of all: Who are we, really?

Living in Illusion

Most people assume, 'I am this body.' They spend their whole lives focused on things like how they look, what they wear, how strong or smart they are and what others think of them. But Krishna teaches us that this is a big illusion.

We are not these temporary bodies—we are eternal spirit souls, tiny parts of God. Right now, we are trapped in a material body, but instead of realizing this and working toward something greater, we get lost in just trying to satisfy the body's basic needs.

Think about it—what do animals do all day? They eat, sleep, mate and defend themselves. That's it. If we live only to chase food, comfort, relationships and security, are we really any different from animals?

The human body is special because it gives us the ability to think beyond these things. We can ask deeper questions:

- Why am I here?
- Is there more to life than just survival and pleasure?
- What happens after death?

But most people never ask these questions. They get stuck in a cycle of temporary pleasures, never realizing their true identity. This is the real problem of life—not hunger, not money, not relationships but forgetting who we truly are.

Krishna's teachings in the Bhagavad Gita wake us up from this illusion and guide us toward a life of real meaning, beyond just eating, sleeping and surviving.

So, the big question is: Do we want to live like everyone else—chasing temporary pleasures—or do we want to discover who we truly are?

The Special Prerogative

As stated in the Hitopadesha (Text 25):

> *āhāra-nidrā-bhaya-maithunaṁ ca*
> *sāmānyam etat paśubhir narāṇām*
> *dharmo hi teṣām adhiko viśeṣo*
> *dharmeṇa hīnaḥ paśubhiḥ samānaḥ*
>
> 'Eating, sleeping, sex, and defence—these four principles are common to both human beings and animals. The distinction between human life and animal life is that a man can search for God, but an animal cannot.'

Thus, to get a human body and not endeavour to lead a God-conscious life in His service is an animal's life.

It is very rare to find a person in this world who is working towards this real purpose of human life. Krishna says among thousands, one may be interested, which is so true as we see in this world today. People are only interested in enjoyment: partying, travelling or thereabouts, but they do not have any interest or time for God.

In fact, they feel it's something outdated, or they simply do not believe in Him, saying there is nothing like God. Faith in God is a blessing bestowed only on the fortunate ones. But even if someone manages to perfect his spiritual journey, it is very difficult for him to know Krishna fully.

The Secret Path of the Soul

Great yogis, even after years of austerities (*tapasya*), or many engaged in cultivating knowledge (*jnana*) or acting piously (leading a sinless life or working for the welfare of society), for many lifetimes, cannot know Krishna. Krishna can only be approached through bhakti (devotional service) and not by any other means. When He is pleased with our sincere service, He reveals Himself. It is impossible to know or see Him through our present material senses:

ataḥ śrī-kṛṣṇa-nāmādi
na bhaved grāhyam indriyaiḥ
sevonmukhe hi jihvādau
svayam eva sphuraty adaḥ

Bhakti Rasamrita Sindhu (1.2.234)

'Material senses cannot understand Krishna's holy name, form, qualities and pastimes. When a conditioned soul is awakened to Krishna consciousness and renders service by using his tongue to chant the Lord's holy name and taste the remnants of the Lord's food, the tongue is purified, and one gradually comes to understand who Krishna really is.'

The method is very simple: devotional service. But where to begin? Service to Krishna begins with the tongue. The tongue has two functions: to taste and to vibrate. Even if we have no knowledge of Him, if we simply use our tongue to taste the prasad (food offered to Krishna), and to chant His holy names under the guidance of a dear devotee of the Lord, then everything about Him will be revealed to us. But such a soul is very rare.

muktānām api siddhānāṁ
nārāyaṇa-parāyaṇaḥ
su-durlabhaḥ praśāntātmā
koṭiṣv api mahā-mune

Shrimad Bhagavatam (6.14.5)

'Among many millions, who are liberated and perfect in knowledge of liberation, one may be a devotee of Lord Narayana or Krishna. Such devotees, who are fully peaceful, are extremely rare.'

Further, it is said in the Bhagavad Gita (7.19):

bahūnāṁ janmanām ante
jñānavān māṁ prapadyante

vāsudevaḥ sarvam iti
sa mahātmā su-durlabhaḥ

'After many births and deaths, he who is actually in knowledge surrenders unto Me, knowing Me to be the cause of all causes and all that is. Such a great soul is very rare.'

Keep it Simple

Thus, in a world where even the greatest minds and ascetics often fail to find Him, Krishna opens Himself only to a heart filled with devotion. Not through intellect, not through ritual but through simple, loving service—beginning with the tongue, chanting His names and honouring His prasad.

Such a path may seem too simple to be profound, but that is Krishna's mercy. The highest truth is hidden in the humblest acts of devotion. And the rarest souls are not those who know everything—but those who serve with sincerity.

To come in contact with a devotee, to hear about Krishna, to chant His name with feeling—this is the turning point of lifetimes. Blessed are those who follow this path.

Anyone who has faith in Krishna and is engaged in His devotional service, even if it's very little, is very fortunate. He is no ordinary soul, and if we are fortunate enough to engage with such souls, we must render humble service to them and be blessed. Just by serving such souls we will acquire the affinity for Krishna's message and gain the highest understanding of the purpose of life.

24

Krishna, the Source

In a world full of competing philosophies and endless debates about who or what is supreme, there stands a voice that echoes through time, clear and unshaken—**Krishna**. Not just another deity among many, not a regional figure in a mythological tale, but the cause of all causes, the thread that holds the universe together, and the ultimate reality behind everything that exists.

He boldly declares in the Bhagavad Gita (7.7) that there is no truth higher than Him:

mattaḥ parataraṁ nānyat
kiñcid asti dhanañ-jaya
mayi sarvam idaṁ protaṁ
sūtre maṇi-gaṇā iva

'O conqueror of wealth, there is no truth superior to Me. Everything rests upon Me, as pearls are strung on a thread.'

Not Ego, But Eternal Truth

Someone may argue, 'Well, by this logic, anyone can claim to be the supreme. Is it not being boastful?

This isn't a claim born of ego, but a revelation confirmed by the greatest sages, saints and scriptures of all time—from Vyasa, the compiler of all Vedic knowledge and ultimate authority on the subject, and Narada to Brahma to Shri Vallabhacharya, Shri Ramanujacharya, Shri Madhvacharya and Shri Shankaracharya. The Vedas, Vedanta and the Bhagavatam all converge on this one truth: Krishna is the Supreme Lord.

Lord Brahma, the first created being, declares the supreme position of Krishna in Brahma Samhita (5.1):

īśvaraḥ paramaḥ kṛṣṇaḥ
sac-cid-ānanda-vigrahaḥ
anādir ādir govindaḥ
sarva-kāraṇa-kāraṇam

'Krishna, who is known as Govinda, is the Supreme Godhead. He has an eternal, blissful spiritual body. He is the origin of all. He has no other origin, and He is the prime cause of all causes.'

Vedanta Speaks

Vedanta means the end of all knowledge. The essence of the knowledge of all the scriptures has been compiled by Shri Vyasadeva in the 'Vedanta Sutra' in the form of aphorisms, wherein he mentions: *janmady asya yatah* (1.1.2)—God is someone from whom everything emanates. And then in the Shrimad Bhagavatam, which is the natural commentary on Vedanta Sutra by the author (Shri Vyasadeva) himself, he introduces who God is in the very first verse itself.

oṁ namo bhagavate vāsudevāya
janmādy asya yato 'nvayād itarataś cārtheṣv
abhijñaḥ svarāṭ
tene brahma hṛdā ya ādi-kavaye muhyanti
yat sūrayaḥ
tejo-vāri-mṛdāṁ yathā vinimayo yatra
tri-sargo 'mṛṣā
dhāmnā svena sadā nirasta-kuhakaṁ satyaṁ
paraṁ dhīmahi

'O my Lord, Shri Krishna, son of Vasudeva, O all-pervading Personality of Godhead, I offer my respectful obeisances unto You. I meditate upon Lord Shri Krishna because He is the Absolute Truth and the primeval cause of all causes of the creation, sustenance and destruction of the manifested universes. He is directly and indirectly conscious of

> all manifestations, and He is independent because there is no other cause beyond Him. It is He only who first imparted the Vedic knowledge unto the heart of Lord Brahma the original living being. By Him even the great sages and demigods are placed into illusion, as one is bewildered by the illusory representations of water seen in fire, or land seen on water. Only because of Him do the material universes, temporarily manifested by the reactions of the three modes of nature, appear factual, although they are unreal. I therefore meditate upon Him, Lord Shri Krishna, who is eternally existent in the transcendental abode, which is forever free from the illusory representations of the material world. I meditate upon Him, for He is the Absolute Truth.'

Shri Vyasadeva clearly indicates that God is none other than the son of Vasudeva. And we all know who the son of Vasudeva is—none other than our dear Lord Krishna. Just to substantiate his point, Vyasadeva includes the '*janmady asya yatah*' verse in this first verse of Shrimad Bhagavatam to convey that the Supreme Lord mentioned in the Vedanta Sutra is the same as the son of Vasudeva. And it is He who is the cause behind the workings of the universe and holding everything together, like a thread in a pearl necklace.

The Invisible Thread

A pearl necklace is beautiful but only as long as all the pearls are held together by the thread. But do we see the thread? We only admire the beauty of the necklace. But it's the thread that makes the necklace look beautiful. As soon as the thread breaks, everything falls apart and the necklace ceases to exist. The very fact that the pearls are together in a systematic way means there is a cause that is holding them together, even though it may not be seen. Similarly, the fact that so many wonderful phenomena are active within the universe, such as seasons changing cyclically, the sun rising from the east and setting in the west and planets moving in their own orbits, is proof that someone is making it happen, though He may not be seen.

An intelligent mind always wonders, what is the cause behind all this? Well, here Krishna answers this once and for all: He Himself is the cause and He is the one holding everything together. No one else in the history of creation has ever made this claim. Thus, we accept Krishna's claim just as many great souls in the past have done.

The Unseen Cause Behind All Seen Effects

When things go haywire, we deduce that no one is in charge, but when things are happening very systematically, we understand that someone is overseeing them, just the way things happening in this world is enough to make us believe that God exists. We do not need to see Him first to believe in Him.

In a puppet show, we see the puppets dancing. The puppeteer is not seen but only a fool would think that puppets are dancing on their own.

When we see an arrow slicing through the air, we don't argue whether someone shot it—we instinctively know there's an archer. When a fan rotates, we don't insist on seeing electricity to believe it's there. We simply acknowledge the effect and accept the cause.

Yet, when we behold the breathtaking complexity of the cosmos—the perfect orbits of planets, the precision of natural laws, the rhythm of seasons, the miracle of life—we hesitate to accept a supreme cause. That is not intelligence; that is denial.

Effect Implies Cause. Order Implies Intelligence. Design Implies a Designer

To deny the existence of Krishna, the Supreme Designer, just because He is not visible to our limited eyes, is like denying the puppeteer while watching the puppets dance.

The greatest illusion is thinking this magnificent creation is self-sustaining without a creator. The greatest awakening is recognizing the invisible hand that holds it all together—Krishna, the ultimate cause of all causes.

The wise don't wait to see Him with their eyes—they recognize Him through His unmistakable signature written all over creation.

We see an arrow being shot and flying through the air. Although the person who shot it may not be seen but, it is still a no-brainer to think that someone has shot it.

We see the fan moving. We do not see the cause, but just seeing the effect makes us aware of the cause: the electricity.

Similarly, just by seeing the beautiful creation that is this world, its order and design and the variety available in it, it is easy to conclude that there is a designer, though He may not be visible to us with our naked eyes in the present moment.

25

The Prison of Illusion (Maya)

Every soul originally belongs to the spiritual world—the eternal kingdom of God, where love, harmony and bliss reign supreme. But when a soul desires to turn away from Krishna, seeking independence and control, that pure existence is interrupted. Just like a citizen who rebels against a righteous government is sent to prison, the soul is sent to the material world—a cosmic rehabilitation centre for those who defy divine order.

This is similar to a city where citizens live in complete harmony with the government. As soon as a citizen tries to act independently of the government or against its will, they are sent to a prison to protect the innocent and prevent disorder in society.

Chasing Pleasure, Finding Sorrow

This world is not our true home. It is a prison-house of illusion, created not out of cruelty but out of mercy—to allow the soul to pursue its misguided desires, learn from the pain that follows and eventually turn back to God.

We come here hoping to enjoy ourselves, but instead we suffer. In place of freedom, we encounter bondage—in the form of birth, old age, disease and death. Added to that are the relentless miseries of the mind, conflicts with others and the unpredictable strikes of nature.

The soul enters this world chasing pleasure but finds only sorrow. Why? Because separation from Krishna is the root cause of all suffering—and the material world is simply the reflection of that broken relationship.

The Role of Durga, the Jailer

This material world, also known as '*durg*', exists under the watchful eyes of Durga Devi. Just as a jailer inflicts punishments upon prisoners to rectify their behaviour and align them with the laws of the government, similarly, Durga Devi punishes rebellious souls by subjecting them to various miseries and keeping them under illusion.

She has the thankless task of keeping insincere souls away from Krishna. However, just as a jailer releases a reformed prisoner before the stipulated sentence ends,

Durga Devi also releases a soul when she sees that it has turned to God and is engaged in devotional service. At that moment, her duty is fulfilled.

Reformation, Not Retribution

The purpose of inflicting suffering upon a prisoner in jail is to reform them. Likewise, Durga Devi's role in this world is to make souls realize that the world is not a happy place and that true happiness lies in returning to God.

Once a soul begins to question whether there is a place free from suffering, it marks the beginning of the end of its existence in the material world. However, breaking free from the illusory energy of the Lord, known as Durga Devi, is extremely difficult because she is Krishna's energy and is as powerful as Krishna Himself.

Surrender: The Way Out

Krishna declares in the Bhagavad Gita (7.14) that only those who surrender to Him—meaning those who engage in His devotional service—can be freed from Durga Devi's control:

daivī hy eṣā guṇa-mayī
mama māyā duratyayā
mām eva ye prapadyante
māyām etāṁ taranti te

> 'This divine energy of Mine, consisting of the three modes of material nature, is difficult to overcome. But those who have surrendered unto Me can easily cross beyond it.'

Surrender means to act according to Krishna's will, and when a soul does so, Krishna orders Durga Devi to release it. That is when the soul's blissful life truly begins, and it embarks on the path of liberation.

It is only due to her influence that, even after hearing the words of great saints, we remain unconvinced that this world is not our real home and that we truly belong to Krishna in the spiritual world. It is only because of her control that we mistakenly think of this miserable material life to be blissful and that there is nothing beyond it. However, as soon as her influence is removed—by the blessings of the Lord and His dear devotees—the truth of the scriptures begins to make sense.

Surrendering to God also means surrendering to His representatives because they carry out His will. We may not be able to see God face to face, but we can connect with His representatives. If we simply surrender to their guidance and sincerely follow their instructions, we will be freed from the clutches of illusory energy, which otherwise, is very difficult to overcome.

If we do not surrender to Krishna and His representative, known as the Guru, our material existence and suffering will continue, life after life, with no escape.

Pray: But Daily

Srila Prabhupada, the founder-acharya of the International Society for Krishna Consciousness (ISKCON), was a highly elevated soul who engaged millions of people in the devotional service of Krishna. One day, in the Los Angeles temple, a devotee saw him standing in front of the deities, praying with tears in his eyes. Surprised, the devotee later asked, 'Srila Prabhupada, what were you praying for? We saw tears in your eyes.'

Srila Prabhupada replied, 'I was praying to the Lord, "Please protect me, so that I may never fall under illusion or into Maya."'

Astonished, the devotee asked, 'Srila Prabhupada, how can you ever fall into Maya or illusion?'

Srila Prabhupada replied, 'Because I pray like this every day, therefore, I will never fall into Maya.'

Similarly, if we pray to Krishna, and ask Him to protect us from His illusory energy, simultaneously engaging in His devotional service and accept the words of His representatives as our life and soul, Krishna will surely protect us. He will save us from the afflictions of Maya and bring us back to our original home in the spiritual world, into His eternal association, after we leave this world to live a life of eternal happiness.

As long as we stay in the world of Maya, we can never truly be happy. The inability to understand this is indicative of us being totally under Durga Devi's influence. The sooner we realize this and turn to Krishna, the better it will be for our well-being.

26

Divine Access

Who Will Stay?

One may wonder that if devotional service to Krishna is so rewarding, why does everyone not come to Krishna? And even after coming in touch, why is everyone not able to continue with determination? It is because they lack the necessary qualifications.

Krishna's Qualification Clause

This has been answered by Krishna in Bhagavad Gita (7.28):

yeṣāṁ tv anta-gataṁ pāpaṁ
janānāṁ puṇya-karmaṇām

te dvandva-moha-nirmuktā
bhajante māṁ dṛḍha-vratāḥ

'Persons who have acted piously in previous lives and in this life and whose sinful actions are completely eradicated are freed from the dualities of delusion, and they engage themselves in My service with determination.'

If we wish to meet the Prime Minister or the President of the country, we cannot just barge in or get close to him as and when we like. We need some qualifications, based on which they would want to meet us. If this is true of a mortal of this world, what to speak of the Supreme Lord, the master of all the worlds, Krishna?

The qualification required to approach Krishna and get attracted to His personality is purity of heart. People who have acted piously in their previous lives, as well as in this life, and whose sinful karmas are negligible are able to come to Krishna's devotional service. And once they have arrived, the purer they are, the more determined they will be to stay on the path.

Divine Access Requires Inner Credentials

Many times, we see that some people come to the path of Krishna bhakti, but after some time, we notice how some leave while some stay longer. The reason simply is the fact that the first category had very little devotional credits from their past life and thus, could not continue on their path; the second kind had some extra credits, due to which they stayed longer. Some others, with enough credits for a lifetime, end up staying on and continue longer than anyone else.

Everything depends on how much we are carrying in our pockets to pay the price. It is not easy to come to this path, and it is just as difficult to stay on, because not everyone can pay the price that devotion demands. If we want to be close to fire and survive, we need to be like fire, else we will be burnt. Likewise, if we wish to get close and stay close to Krishna, we need to be pure enough.

Real Diamonds Have Few Buyers

When we sell real diamonds, there will be very few takers but if we sell imitation diamonds that are cheap, many will come. The path of devotional service to Krishna is a rare diamond and if we get it, we must somehow work hard to purchase it and keep it. It is not ordinary.

Two Ways to Krishna

Srila Rupa Goswami, a great Vaishnava Acharya, mentions two basic reasons behind a person's becoming a Krishna devotee:

1. A previous lifetime's devotional credits that a person carried into this life and
2. A devotee's intervention in a person's life.

If a person has acted piously and was fortunate enough to receive the mercy of a dear devotee of the Lord, he begins to perform devotional service. Whatever devotional credits he thus acquires, he carries into this life and begins from where he left off.

Devotees, the Greatest Hope

However, if it was only dependent on a previous lifetime's credits, then what about those who are not carrying any? Will they never become fortunate enough? Will they keep gliding into a deep dark well of ignorance and suffer more and more, life after life?

For people like these, Krishna has made a provision of a devotee's intervention. Even if a person is not carrying any devotional credits, if for one reason or the other, he comes in touch with a devotee of the Lord and receives his blessings, he will receive devotional credits that will help him get attracted to and engage in the all-auspicious path of bhakti, opening the doors to liberation.

But the most important point to note in both the cases is the devotee's mercy. In essence, without receiving the grace of the devotee of a Lord, it is impossible to get Krishna's grace, because that is the system He has authorized. He distributes His grace only through His devotee. Simply being a good, pious soul is not enough.

Stay Pure

If we are pious and pure, we might have greater opportunities to come into the association of saintly devotees, because purity attracts purity. But then, we need to receive their grace by hearing from them the transcendental message and glories of the Lord and humbly serving them. Thus, piety is a step and not the culmination. We must try to be in the good books of a dear devotee of the Lord. As soon as that happens, we will instantly be recognized by Krishna. In fact, He showers more mercy on the devotees of His devotees than His direct devotees. Even if we cannot ever become devotees, we should try to become devotees of the devotees, and our life will be a success.

Mrigari was a cruel hunter. Due to his past karmas, he was born into a family of hunters. But his training as a hunter was unique. He was trained to kill the birds and animals halfway, and not fully, and then enjoy seeing them slowly die, moaning in pain. That was his occupation, and he took great pleasure in it, until one day, the great sage Narada's merciful glance fell upon him. Narada reformed him through his instructions, and by engaging him in Lord Krishna's devotional service by chanting His holy names:

Hare Krishna, Hare Krishna, Krishna Krishna, Hare Hare/Hare Rama, Hare Rama, Rama Rama, Hare Hare

Mrigari became such a pure soul that he did not even want to hurt an ant. This is the power of the mercy of the devotee. Mrigari would have glided to the lowest regions of hell and suffered eternally. He had no qualification, but the mercy of a devotee elevated him and turned him into a saintly soul.

An Earnest Appeal

In this dark age of Kaliyuga, most do not carry any devotional credits, and atheism is becoming more and more rampant. As a result, most need the grace of the dear devotees of the Lord. Thus, it is the duty of each and every devotee of the Lord to make all efforts to reach out to each and every soul, beg them to give up their immoral, sinful lifestyle and engage in the service of Krishna, primarily chanting and hearing His pure names and listening to His beautiful pastimes. And also a humble appeal to everyone in society to support such selfless endeavours of the devotees. This will create everyone's good fortune. Otherwise, everyone is destined to suffer and get degraded more and more, never to come out of this vicious cycle.

27

Destination of the Soul

Imagine closing your eyes for the last time, only to open them somewhere entirely new. A tunnel of light? A vast endless void? A land full of happiness with countless other souls? A return to a life we don't remember?

What if we were told that when we die, our journey is not over, but only just beginning? Some say the soul ascends to a place beyond the stars, others believe it lingers among the living and a few whisper that it is reborn, starting all over again. But where does it really go?

Krishna's Law of Transmigration

Across cultures and centuries, people have claimed to glimpse the soul's next destination. But what really happens when we leave this world? Lord Krishna, the supreme, omniscient master answers this in just a few words in the Bhagavad Gita (8.6):

> *yaṁ yaṁ vāpi smaran bhāvaṁ*
> *tyajaty ante kalevaram*
> *taṁ tam evaiti kaunteya*
> *sadā tad-bhāva-bhāvitaḥ*

> 'Whatever state of being one remembers when he quits his body, O son of Kuntī, that state he will attain without fail.'

The last thoughts of a person decide his next destination: his next family, place of birth and type of body. And the last thoughts will depend on what a person has carried in his thoughts all his life.

Life Is a Preparation, Death Is the Test

Life is a preparation; death is the examination. How well a student has studied will be tested at the time of the final exam. If he passes the final exam, only then are his efforts considered successful, else they are of no use. A student can sit with his books all the time and claim to study, but the final exam will show how serious he was. Similarly, so many people live and claim to have lived a successful life by acquiring name, fame, wealth and engaging in good deeds, or even practising a spiritual life, but how does one define a successful life? It's when a person passes the final exam with flying colours. And what is the passing criteria?

The Real Success

Shrimad Bhagavatam (2.1.6) emphatically declares:

etāvān sāṅkhya-yogābhyāṁ
sva-dharma-pariniṣṭhayā
janma-lābhaḥ paraḥ puṁsām
ante nārāyaṇa-smṛtiḥ

'The highest perfection of human life, achieved either by complete knowledge of matter and spirit, by practice of mystic powers or by perfect discharge of occupational duty, is to remember the Personality of Godhead at the end of life.'

The passing criteria is to think of the Supreme Lord Krishna at the last moment. If the last thoughts are that of Krishna, we are liberated and are sent on our way to Him in the spiritual world, never to return to this world of birth and death. He says in the Bhagavad Gita (8.5):

anta-kāle ca mām eva
smaran muktvā kalevaram
yaḥ prayāti sa mad-bhāvaṁ
yāti nāsty atra saṁśayaḥ

> 'And whoever, at the end of his life, quits his body remembering Me alone at once attains My nature. Of this there is no doubt.'

The USP of the Human Body

As per the Vedic scriptures, there are eighty-four lakh species of life within the universe. That means a soul can get any of these 8.4 million types of bodies based on its desires and subsequent activities. Each body is suited for a particular purpose and out of all, the human birth is considered most rare since only as a human being do we have the best opportunity to put an end to this cycle of birth and death; to stop the transmigration of the soul and get liberated to return to our real home in the spiritual world, thus putting an end to all our suffering.

So, if a person is able to get liberated as a human being or utilizes his life to attain this goal, it is understood that he has attained the success of his human birth. He has achieved what this human body was given to him for.

Remembrance Is the Key

In the above-mentioned verses, the word *smaran* ('remembering') is important. Remembrance of Krishna is not possible for the impure soul, who has not practiced remembering Him throughout his life.

Therefore, one should practice Krishna consciousness from the very beginning of life. If one wants to achieve success at the end of his life, the process of remembering Krishna is essential.

The recommended process in this Yuga is very simple: one should constantly, incessantly chant the maha-mantra—*Hare Krishna, Hare Krishna, Krishna Krishna, Hare Hare/Hare Rama, Hare Rama, Rama Rama, Hare Hare*. There may be so many impediments for a person who is chanting Hare Krishna. Nonetheless, tolerating all these impediments, one should continue to chant the holy names of Krishna so that at the end of one's life, one can have the full benefit of devotional service to the Lord. The Lord has invested all His blessings, power and divine grace in His names. If we chant them, we will be able to remember Him always, especially at the end of our life. Else, we are in a great danger of losing the valuable opportunity as a human being.

Watch Your Attachments

Instead of becoming attached to God, people are cultivating various undue material attachments, including those to other living beings apart from humans. But we must know that there is a proper place for everything in life, and whatever we get attached to will occupy our thoughts. Thus, we must be very careful about where our attachments are.

King Bharata, although a great personality, thought of a deer at the end of his life, and so in his next life he was transferred into the body of a deer. Although as a deer he remembered his past activities, he had to accept that animal body. Hence, the last thoughts are important.

But one's thoughts during the course of one's life accumulate to influence one's thoughts at the moment of death, so this life creates one's next life. Whatever we have given our time and energy to throughout our life is what we will think of at the last moment. If in one's present life one lives in the mode of goodness and spends some time every day to think of Krishna, it is possible for one to remember Him at the end of one's life. That will help one be transferred to the transcendental abode of Krishna, having fulfilled the goal of human life.

Become Absorbed in Krishna

If one is transcendentally absorbed in Krishna's service, then his next body will be transcendental (spiritual), not material. Therefore, the chanting of *Hare Krishna, Hare Krishna, Krishna Krishna, Hare Hare/Hare Rama, Hare Rama, Rama Rama, Hare Hare* is the best and easiest process for successfully changing one's state of being to a higher one at the end of one's life.

As we chant this mantra daily and hear its vibration, our thoughts begin to change and become more focussed on the Lord. Any moment could be the last one. Thus, the goal should be to live our life in such a way that as and when that crucial moment comes, we can remember Krishna and pass the final exam to perfect our human life.

28

The Messy World

An intelligent person is one who works towards ending the real problems of life. True intelligence is not measured by how well one can earn money, score in exams or navigate worldly affairs. While these may impress society, they do little to address the root issues of human existence. An intelligent person looks beyond temporary gains and seeks lasting solutions. He or she doesn't just patch up surface problems but digs deeper to ask: *Why do I suffer? Why do I age, fall sick and die? Why am I forced to take birth again and again in this unpredictable world?*

Real vs Relative Problems

The problems are of two types:

1. **Relative:** What is a problem for one person may not be a problem for others or may even be a source of happiness for someone else—something like 'one man's food is another's poison'—and may keep changing as per the time, place and circumstances.

Take festivals, for instance, where, owing to eating a lot of sweets, there might be a long queue of patients moaning in pain outside the dentist's clinic; but the dentist might be jumping in joy due to having so many patients so that he can earn more. Similarly, during the rainy season, a vegetable seller might be in distress, but an umbrella seller is in bliss.

2. **Real:** A problem that falls in the following categories:
   - It is common to all,
   - No one wants it and
   - No one can avoid it.

As per Vedic literature, there are four real problems of life: birth, old age, disease and death.

Every sane man should think about how to put an end to these problems. Every other problem is a subset of these real problems. Human life is especially meant to stop these miseries. They come as a part of the package of the world we live in where, as described by Krishna, everything is **temporary** and **full of misery,** or where misery is more prominent.

He states in the Bhagavad Gita (8.15):

mām upetya punar janma
duḥkhālayam aśāśvatam
nāpnuvanti mahātmānaḥ
saṁsiddhiṁ paramāṁ gatāḥ

'After attaining Me, the great souls, who are yogīs in devotion, never return to this temporary world, which is full of miseries, because they have attained the highest perfection.'

A Fool's Paradise

Only fools find this world to be a happy place. Even within the so-called happiness here, there is a seed of distress. Everything we work hard for—our business, money, health, family, love—will one day be taken away from us, against our will.

And we call this a happy place? We are forced to grow old, we get diseased and we die and we still find this world a happy place? Someone may say that all this is a part of life, so what? Well, no. We are not supposed to be going through any misery. We are eternal, spiritual beings full of bliss. We go through pain because we are in a foreign land which, by nature, is a land of perpetual suffering. We belong to the spiritual world where life is eternal, full of knowledge and bliss, but since we have come to this material world, we are bound by its laws, and we think this is life.

Even if someone says, 'I do not believe in all these things and I'm happy the way I am.'—well, even then you cannot deny the fact that you cannot live like this forever, and one day you will have to leave this world and go somewhere. So, why not aim for the best place? Why come back to a place where everything has a shelf life? Why not aim for a place where there is no anxiety, old age, disease or death, and there is no separation from our loved ones? Is it not intelligence? We have to leave, so why not seek and prepare for the best realm?

Someone might say that if not here, I will go enjoy the heavenly planets. To them, Krishna replies, 'All places within this material world, right from the topmost planet of Lord Brahma down to the lowest, are places of misery where repeated birth and death takes place.'

ā-brahma-bhuvanāl lokāḥ
punar āvartino 'rjuna
mām upetya tu kaunteya
punar janma na vidyate

Bhagavad Gita (8.16)

'From the highest planet in the material world down to the lowest, all are places of misery wherein repeated birth and death take place. But one who attains to My abode, O son of Kuntī, never takes birth again.'

The Spiritual World: A Motivation to Exit

Once we reach the Supreme Lord's abode—Vaikuntha, or Goloka Vrindavan—we do not come back to this messy place.

> *avyakto 'kṣara ity uktas*
> *tam āhuḥ paramāṁ gatim*
> *yaṁ prāpya na nivartante*
> *tad dhāma paramaṁ mama*
>
> *Bhagavad Gita (8.21)*

> 'That which the Vedāntists describe as unmanifest and infallible, that which is known as the supreme destination, that place from which, having attained it, one never returns—that is My supreme abode.'

By describing the miserable nature of this world, Krishna is trying to inspire us to get out of here. He, being the Creator, obviously knows more about His creation than any of us. It is only due to the illusions that we consider this world to be a nice place.

And all this talk is not to make us feel depressed. It is to help us find a better place to live forever. Everyone wants to live happily ever after. But as long as we are in this world, 'happily ever after' will never be possible because this is called '*Mrityuloka*': a world of death (*mrityu*). Death ends everything, so what can we say of other miseries during our lifetime, such as those caused by mind and body, by others and by natural calamities?

In fact, we do not find even a single good adjective in the scriptures for the world we live in. Somewhere, it has been described as '*karagar*' (jail), deep dark well, 'durg' (an impenetrable fort), '*bhava sagar*' (unfathomable ocean) and so on. We should live in such a way that we do not have to return to this place. And the way out is Krishna. If we worship Him during our lifetime, we go to His abode by His divine grace.

Krishna's Urgent Invitation to Leave

Krishna promises in the Bhagavad Gita (8.8):

> *abhyāsa-yoga-yuktena*
> *cetasā nānya-gāminā*
> *paramaṁ puruṣaṁ divyaṁ*
> *yāti pārthānucintayan*

> 'He who meditates on Me as the Supreme Lord, his mind constantly engaged in remembering Me, undeviated from the path, he, O Partha, is sure to reach Me.'

We must prioritize our spiritual life centred around Krishna because He is Mukunda, the giver of mukti or liberation. Life is unpredictable and anything can happen anytime. We must not wait till old age to take our spiritual life seriously. We have got this valuable human life. Let us not miss this opportunity. Let it be our last birth in the material world. Let us aim to not come back. Let us take our next birth in the spiritual world where every word is a song, every step a dance, every day a festival that absorbs our minds in the praise of the Lord and His companions.

The Beauty of the Spiritual World

The great Vaishnava poet, Shri Narottama Dasa Thakur, has beautifully described the spiritual abode of Krishna in order to increase our greed to go there. He writes:

(1)
vṛndāvana ramya-sthāna dibya-ciṅtāmaṇi-dhāma
ratana mandira manohara
abṛta kālindī-nīre rāja-haṁsa keli kare
tāhe śobhe kanaka-kamal

(2)
tār madhye hema-pīṭha aṣṭa-dale beṣṭita
aṣṭa-dale pradhāna nāyika
tār madhye ratnāsane ba'si āchen dui-jane
śyāma-saṅge sundarī rādhikā

(3)
o-rūpa-lābaṇya-rāśi amiyā pariche khasi
hāsya-parihāsa-sambhāṣaṇe

narottama-dāsa koy nitya-līlā sukha-moy
sadāi sphurūk mora mane

(1)
'Beautiful Vrindavana is filled with *chintamani* (wish-fulfilling) gems and many jewelled palaces and temples. Many regal swans play in the waters of the Yamuna, and in those waters, a splendid golden lotus flower grows.'

(2)
'In the middle of that lotus is a golden place surrounded by eight petals. On these eight petals, the eight principal Gopis reside, and in the centre Lord Syamasundara (Krishna) and beautiful Shri Radharani sit on a jewelled throne.'

(3)
'The great beauty of the Divine Couple and Their charming banter and laughter continually showers nectar everywhere. Narottama Dasa says: "I pray that these blissful eternal transcendental pastimes of the Divine Couple may be always manifested in my heart."'

Our feet might be in the material world right now, but we must keep our eyes on the spiritual world to be able to get there. And, for that, we must remind ourselves of its beauty, every day!

29

When Fools Judge the Divine

We have a tendency to impose our consciousness and shortcomings on others. We see others not as they are, but as we are. Unfortunately, we end up applying this rule to God, too, when He decides to come to this world. Krishna calls such people fools, as they consider Him to be ordinary like them, as He declares in the Bhagavad Gita (9.11):

avajānanti māṁ mūḍhā
mānuṣīṁ tanum āśritam
paraṁ bhāvam ajānanto
mama bhūta-maheśvaram

'Fools deride Me when I descend in the human form. They do not know My transcendental nature as the Supreme Lord of all that be.'

The Extraordinary Appears as the Ordinary

When the Lord descends to this world, He may appear like us, but His form is not ordinary, as Lord Brahma describes in the Brahma Samhita (5.1):

īśvaraḥ paramaḥ krishnaḥ
sac-cid-ānanda-vigrahaḥ
anādir ādir govindaḥ
sarva-kāraṇa-kāraṇam

> 'Krishna, who is known as Govinda, is the Supreme Godhead. He has an eternal blissful spiritual body. He is the origin of all. He has no other origin, and He is the prime cause of all causes.'

The Lord has a form that is transcendental and not material. He does not age like us. He may perform activities like us, but He is above us all. God is God in all situations, and He is not bound by any rules, just as a king is not bound by any rules. When He descends to this world, He performs uncommon activities, but people with a few grams of brain substance misunderstand His actions and dare to find fault with Him.

The Karmic Implications

The law of karma states that if we talk ill of somebody, we will get a reaction for that karma. So, what can we say of talking ill of God? Please remember, the reaction will be extremely severe. When the Lord comes to this world and performs His activities, we may not understand why He does what He does, because it may feel like a mystery to us, but there is a difference between saying 'I don't understand' and 'I don't like or accept'.

The first is a statement of humility and thus, healthy for our life, but the second is a statement full of pride. The Lord's activities are called *leela*, and our actions are called karma. Our every word and action has a reaction. When words and actions are directed at God, the rewards and punishment will be more than proportionate.

The Fault Lies with Our Vision

This world is a drama stage for the Lord. A drama is performed for two reasons: to entertain and enlighten (to convey a message). When the Lord comes to this world, He indulges in activities to entertain His devotees and enlighten non-devotees. Therefore, it is called leela. Leela means something that is done for the sake of enjoyment, pleasure and to teach somebody something. There is no selfish desire to be fulfilled by the Lord because He is self-satsified. Thus there cannot be any fault in Him.

People with a demoniac nature and without faith find faults in the Lord's actions, such as dancing in the

Raas Leela, stealing butter and so on. The Raas Leela was performed by Krishna to please His devotees, the Gopis, as per their desire. Krishna stole butter as a child to please the Gopis of Vrindavan as they wanted Krishna to come and steal their butter and, in the process, also steal their hearts. There can be no fault in God, otherwise, the very purpose of being God gets defeated. The fault lies in our vision.

Only Devotion Can Open the Eyes

The only method to understand Krishna and what He does and says is through devotion, as He Himself declares in the Bhagavad Gita (18.55):

bhaktyā mām abhijānāti
yāvān yaś cāsmi tattvataḥ
tato māṁ tattvato jñātvā
viśate tad-anantaram

'One can understand Me as I am, as the Supreme Personality of Godhead, only by devotional service. And when one is in full consciousness of Me by such devotion, he can enter into the kingdom of God.'

Further, He says in the Bhagavad Gita (11.54):

bhaktyā tv ananyayā śakya
aham evaṁ-vidho 'rjuna

jñātuṁ draṣṭuṁ ca tattvena
praveṣṭuṁ ca paran-tapa

'My dear Arjuna, only by undivided devotional service can I be understood as I am, standing before you, and can thus be seen directly. Only in this way can you enter into the mysteries of My understanding.'

One who has devotion or love for the Lord will understand His activities. Duryodhana had Krishna right next to him, seeing Him regularly, but since he lacked devotion, he could not understand Krishna's supreme position and considered Him to be some ordinary magician; whereas a simple household lady like Vidurani, the wife of Vidura, could understand Krishna's position.

Ravana lacked devotion, and he could not understand the supremacy of Lord Ram; but his youngest brother, Vibhishana, could easily understand Lord Ram as the Supreme Lord.

To further prove His divinity, Krishna declares in the Bhagavad Gita (4.6):

ajo 'pi sann avyayātmā
bhūtānām īśvaro 'pi san
prakṛtiṁ svām adhiṣṭhāya
sambhavāmy ātma-māyayā

> 'Although I am unborn and My transcendental body never deteriorates, and although I am the Lord of all living entities, by My internal energy I still appear in every millennium in My original transcendental form.'

He does not change His body like us, nor does He die. He is eternal and the master of the three worlds in all circumstances. Whenever He appears in this world, He appears out of His own sweet will and in the self-same body.

The Everlasting Glory of Krishna's Pastimes

If Krishna were ordinary, then why would poets be singing praises of Him even after 5000 years? Why would they be composing songs about simple activities, such as stealing butter and dancing with the Gopis of Vrindavan?

Nobody is singing about us or our activities, however good they might seem externally. The proof that Krishna is not ordinary is that everything He does is not ordinary. Therefore, everything He has done has become a celebration forever. He definitely is not an ordinary person. Krishna stole butter and danced with the Gopis, but He also lifted the mighty Govardhan Hill and danced on the hood of Kaliya. Thus, can he be ordinary?

Selective Belief Is Intellectual Dishonesty

Someone might say that's not true and it's simply some imagination at work. But ponder a little—the same scripture that talks about Krishna stealing butter and dancing with the Gopis also talks about Krishna dancing on the hood of the snake Kaliya and lifting Govardhan Hill. Why are we so conveniently accepting one part and rejecting the other? If we must accept, we should accept everything or nothing. As one great saint said, 'You either be hot or be cold. If you are lukewarm, I will spit you out.' Either become a complete atheist or a complete theist. Lukewarm people have no value.

People find faults with Lord Ram, saying that He left Mother Sita. But the same Ram also took on the mighty Ravana to save her and built a bridge over an ocean, a feat that has never been equalled by anybody in the history of creation. If Lord Ram's activities were ordinary, they wouldn't be sung about even after centuries with so much love and devotion.

Humilty Is the Gateway

God's actions, though sometimes beyond our understanding, are never without purpose. Everything the Lord does is meant to either enlighten us or elevate us. What seems unfair or confusing is simply a reflection of our limited vision, not a flaw in His divine plan.

Rather than blame or reject what we don't understand, the intelligent path is one of humility. When a child can't grasp the wisdom of a parent, it is not the parent who is wrong—it is the child who must grow. Similarly, when we fail to understand the Lord's actions, we must not declare Him wrong; we must admit that *we don't yet see the full picture.*

The Vedic path does not demand blind faith—it invites humble inquiry. If we don't understand Krishna's actions, we should not jump to arrogant conclusions. Instead of saying 'I don't accept it' or 'He's at fault', we should simply become humble and accept that we are ignorant and cannot understand the real reason behind the actions. We must then approach His devoted servants, who carry the torchlight of knowledge. It is through their guidance that our doubts dissolve and our hearts open to the beauty and logic of the Lord's ways.

So let us not waste time judging the infinite through our finite lenses. Let us strive to understand. Let us purify our hearts. Let us hear from those who know. That is the sign of real intelligence—and the beginning of real peace.

30

Remembrance

The Soul's Lifeline in Chaos

The Vedic scriptures, which are the law books for humanity, mention many rules or regulative principles to be followed by all human beings to lead a meaningful life. But there are two rules that are known as the kings of all the rules, and if we follow these two, we are understood to be following all. They are mentioned in the Padma Purana (Uttara Khanda, 71.113):

smartavyaḥ satataṁ viṣṇur
vismartavyo na jātucit
sarve vidhi-niṣedhāḥ syur
etayor eva kiṅkarāḥ

Padma Purana

'Krishna is the origin of Lord Viṣṇu. He should always be remembered and never forgotten at any time. All the rules and prohibitions mentioned in the scriptures should be the servants of these two principles.'

Krishna Personally Takes Care

One who always remembers Krishna with undivided attention will have all his needs personally fulfilled by Him and be protected from all types of calamities. There is no doubt about it. He has promised in the Bhagavad Gita (9.22):

ananyāś cintayanto māṁ
ye janāḥ paryupāsate
teṣāṁ nityābhiyuktānāṁ
yoga-kṣemaṁ vahāmy aham

'But those who always worship Me with exclusive devotion, meditating on My transcendental form—to them I carry what they lack, and I preserve what they have.'

The Power of Remembrance

Remembrance (*smaranam*) is the key. It is the most powerful sutra (principle) for life. If we ever feel stuck anywhere in life and things seem to be falling apart, or we are in the middle of some fearful situation or anticipating the same, instead of worrying too much, we should simply bring Krishna's beautiful form into our mind and thus, start remembering Him. We will miraculously see things falling into place. This principle has never failed and will never ever fail.

When Tradition Was Stronger Than Technology

It is only in the last two or three decades that things have taken a different turn and people have moved away from scriptural guidance. Until some years ago, everyone knew that whenever we are in trouble, we only have to start remembering the Lord. When Krishna's father was away in Mathura and realized his child Krishna could be in danger in Gokul, he simply took shelter of the Lord by remembering Him. He did not know that his son was the Supreme Lord Himself, but he followed the principle as it was the only right thing to do.

But now, people simply depend on their own abilities or the abilities of some other who promises to heal them. No one except the Supreme Lord can really help us in life. As soon as we remember Him, all closed doors open and calamities that are to come into our lives due to our past karmas are warded off.

People have countless desires and are constantly running around to fulfil them. In addition, they are in constant anxiety for what they do not have and to protect what they have.

When little devotee Prahalad's life was in danger, he did not even pray for protection. All he did was to simply remember the Lord and he remained unharmed. Even the mighty demon Hiranyakashipu, who was controlling the powerful rulers of the universe, could not do anything to him.

Mishap to Musical Magic: When Krishna Took Over

Magic happens when we remember Krishna. A tragedy turns into an opportunity and a curse turns into a blessing. I have personally experienced this in my own life and have seen others experience the same.

A few years ago, I used to organize a monthly event in Mumbai with the intention of providing people a practical experience of spirituality. In this age of Kali, the recommended spiritual practice is sankirtana—the congregational chanting of the Lord's holy names. With this in mind, a group of devotees and I would host a musical evening where we sang kirtans and concluded with a short talk and final chanting session.

One evening, our regular sound system operator was unavailable, and we had to hire someone else. The event had a gathering of nearly 120 people. Midway through the programme, a few well-known singers arrived as special guests, but they could only stay for twenty minutes. We gladly gave them the stage, and as they completed their kirtan, an unexpected mishap occurred—a microphone slipped from someone's hand and hit the ground, causing the entire sound system to trip.

I was seated next to the sound system operator and could see him frantically working to fix the issue. Inside, I felt a surge of anxiety. The entire event depended on the sound system, and without it, everything could fall apart. However, I made a conscious effort not to express any distress externally. Instead, I turned inward and started remembering our beloved Shri Shri Radha Gopinath. I focused on Him with complete surrender, asking for His guidance, while outwardly maintaining a calm demeanour.

I could sense the audience's confusion and restlessness as they waited for the issue to be resolved. Then, suddenly, an idea struck me. I felt an inexplicable surge of energy coursing through my body. Without hesitation, I turned to the audience and said, 'The sound system isn't working, but that doesn't mean we have to stop. How about I pick up the harmonium and sit among all of you? Let's gather closely and chant together.'

The audience, rather than being disappointed, responded with enthusiasm. They immediately adjusted their seating, forming a few intimate circles around me. A couple of devotee musicians sat beside me, and we began to sing. It was 6.30 p.m. when we started. As we lost ourselves in the kirtan, time seemed to dissolve. When I finally stopped, it was 7.30 p.m.—

an entire hour had passed without anyone realizing it. The expressions on everyone's faces were priceless. Their eyes were wide open in astonishment, and they exclaimed, 'Is it over already? Can't we continue for a little longer?'

We had hosted countless kirtans before, but that evening was different. Everyone unanimously said that it was the most divine and powerful experience they had ever had.

Among the attendees was a psychiatrist from London. After the event, she came up to me and shared her experience. She admitted that at one point, she was sceptical about how things would proceed. But the moment I got up and took charge, she could feel the entire energy in the hall shift. She had never experienced something so transcendental before, and she marvelled at how quickly that one hour had passed.

I knew exactly how it had happened. Externally, the situation was far from ideal—without a proper sound system or a formal stage setup. But inwardly, the moment I surrendered to Radha-Krishna, everything changed. What could have been a disaster transformed into an unforgettable, divine experience.

This is just one of many such experiences in my life where I have witnessed the incredible power of remembering Krishna. The more we take shelter in Him, the more we realize that He is the ultimate controller, turning every difficulty into an opportunity for transcendence. Never underestimate the power of heartfelt remembrance of the Lord—it has the ability to change lives in ways we cannot even imagine.

Another Wonderful Incident:

The Verse That Invited a Miracle

Arjunacharya and his wife were simple and humble devotees, living in a small hut. Each day, after completing his morning duties, Arjunacharya would go to the village to beg for alms. He visited only three houses each day, accepting just enough alms to sustain himself and his wife. When not begging, he spent his hours reading and writing a commentary on the Bhagavad Gita.

One day, deeply engrossed in his work, Arjunacharya forgot to go to the village for food. Realizing it was already late afternoon, he hurried out but found no food, as the women in the village were resting. He returned home empty-handed and resumed his study of the Bhagavad Gita.

In the Chapter 9, verse 22, Lord Krishna promises:

ananyāś cintayanto māṁ
ye janāḥ paryupāsate
teṣāṁ nityābhiyuktānāṁ
yoga-kṣemaṁ vahāmy aham

> 'But those who always worship Me with exclusive devotion, meditating on My transcendental form — to them I carry what they lack, and I preserve what they have.'

Arjunacharya doubted this statement and scratched out the line, questioning how the Lord could personally carry anything.

Leaving for a bath, Arjunacharya missed the arrival of two boys (Krishna and Balarama) at his home. They carried loads of rice, vegetables, fruits and butter, and handed them to Arjunacharya's wife, saying they were disciples of her husband. She was delighted but noticed scars on their backs. The boys claimed that her husband made them work hard and beat them if they disobeyed.

When Arjunacharya returned, his wife confronted him, accusing him of mistreating the boys. Shocked and confused, he realized the boys were Krishna and Balarama. He rushed to his Bhagavad Gita and found the scratches he made on the shloka had vanished. Overcome with emotion, he wept, realizing the truth of the Lord's words and His personal care for His devotees.

Trust Every Word

Each and every word spoken in the scriptures is the absolute truth and anyone who doubts this will miss out on a wonderful blessing. All we need is a leap of faith.

So, the next time you have any '*chinta*' (worry), start doing '*chintan*' (remembrance of the Lord) and see your 'chinta' disappear magically. If Krishna has promised that He will provide what we lack and protect what we have if we sincerely remember Him, He certainly will.

We must act in a way that we always remember Krishna, and we must refrain from doing things that make us forget Him. This is the secret to success in every endeavour.

31

Different Paths, Different Destinations

If you board a flight to Bengaluru, you will not land in Delhi. If you eat junk food, your body will not reward you with the benefits of a healthy diet. Simple logic—every action leads to a corresponding result. Yet, when it comes to spirituality, many people abandon this logic and begin believing that '*all paths lead to the same goal*'.

But just as not all roads lead to the same city, not all forms of worship lead to the same destination. The intention, the object of worship and the consciousness behind it all determine what benefits we achieve.

The Ultimate Verdict

Krishna Himself settles this debate clearly and emphatically in the Bhagavad Gita (9.25):

yānti deva-vratā devān
pitṝn yānti pitṛ-vratāḥ
bhūtāni yānti bhūtejyā
yānti mad-yājino 'pi mām

'Those who worship the demigods will take birth among the demigods; those who worship the ancestors go to the ancestors; those who worship ghosts and spirits will take birth among such beings; and those who worship Me will live with Me.'

In one verse, the Lord destroys the illusion of spiritual relativism. Not all worship is equal. Not all destinations are the same. Not all goals are eternal. Where we place our devotion determines where we ultimately go.

This chapter explores why Krishna alone is the ultimate goal, and why worship of anyone else—no matter how respected—can never give the eternal result that devotion to Him offers.

Suppose a person is washing vessels at a small roadside dhaba or restaurant, while another person is washing vessels for the wealthiest man in the city. Do we think both receive the same benefits? No way. The activity remains the same, yet the rewards depend on whom they are working for.

Similarly, when it comes to worshipping different exalted personalities within the realms of creation, the rewards depend on the destination—on whom we worship.

The Power and Limitation of Worship

If we worship the celestial gods, we go to the heavenly planets, but eventually, we fall back into this material world to continue the cycle of birth and death. If we worship ghosts, we become like them. But if we worship Krishna, we attain His association and remain in His eternal abode. It is as simple as that.

It may sound broad-minded to say that everything is one, that all are the same and that we should not discriminate. However, when we want to send our children to school, why do we discriminate so much? Why do we take so much time to decide which school to send them to? If all schools are the same, why not send them to any random one?

When we sit down to eat, why are we so particular about our food? If everything is the same, why don't we simply eat whatever is on the table—whether it is bitter gourd or a milk sweet?

When we invest, why don't we invest in anything randomly, keeping the same logic of everything is the same in mind? The fact of the matter is that both consciously and subconsciously, we know that everything is not the same. That is why we differentiate and make careful choices. But why is this logic abandoned when it comes to spirituality?

Everything is not one, and not all types of worship yield the same result. Therefore, we must choose carefully. At the same time, nothing will be imposed upon us. However, we should always remember that the amount and quality of grace we receive depends upon whom we worship.

A worshipper of the demigods or celestial beings will not attain liberation and reach Krishna; he will go to the demigods and then fall back into this world. Only devotion to Krishna guarantees liberation and eternal association with Him in the spiritual world.

A Ray of Hope

However, since not everyone is on the same wavelength in life, one must understand that if he remains faithful, sincere and selfless in his worship of his chosen deity, he will eventually come to the right understanding and realize who is truly worthy of worship.

That understanding is summed up in the verse, Bhagavad Gita(7.19):

Vasudevaḥ sarvam iti sa mahātmā su-durlabhaḥ

'Such a great soul is very rare.'

Whatever level we are at, we should faithfully worship and offer our devotion to the deity dear to our heart, praying for guidance toward the most auspicious path. We should try and not ask for anything material but simply offer our worship as an act of gratitude and duty. When we do so, they will happily take us by the hand, bless us with the highest understanding and lead us to the ultimate treasure.

The Touchstone

There was once a Brahmana, who sincerely worshipped Lord Shiva. Pleased with his devotion, Lord Shiva appeared before him one day and offered him a boon.

The Brahmana humbly requested a touchstone. Lord Shiva, surprised at his request, thought, 'Such a pure-hearted Brahmana—what will he do with a mere touchstone? Let me guide him to something even greater.'

Lord Shiva directed him to a saintly personality in Vrindavan known as Sanatana Goswami, who possessed a touchstone.

The Brahmana eagerly approached Sanatana Goswami, who was deeply absorbed in chanting the holy names of Krishna. When asked about the touchstone, Sanatana Goswami casually pointed to a pile of garbage and said, 'It is over there.'

The Brahmana searched through the garbage and, sure enough, found a beautiful touchstone. Overjoyed, he picked it up and started dancing in delight on his way home.

However, a sudden thought struck him: If this touchstone, which can turn anything into gold, was lying in a pile of garbage, then surely this saint must possess something even more valuable! I must go back and ask him for that.

He returned to Sanatana Goswami and requested, 'Please give me that which is even more valuable than this touchstone.'

Sanatana Goswami smiled and said, 'If you truly desire it, then first throw the touchstone into the River Yamuna.'

Without hesitation, the Brahmana cast the touchstone into the river and returned. Seeing his sincerity, Sanatana Goswami gifted him the real touchstone—the holy names of Krishna.

Hare Krishna, Hare Krishna, Krishna Krishna,
Hare Hare/Hare Rama, Hare Rama, Rama Rama,
Hare Hare

The scriptures explain: Nāma-chintāmaṇiḥ Krishnaḥ—the holy name of Krishna is the true touchstone. An ordinary touchstone may turn iron into gold, but the holy name of Krishna can transform even the most fallen soul into the most exalted personality, capable of purifying the entire world.

This is why Lord Shiva, being extremely pleased with the Brahmana, gave him what was closest to his heart—Krishna, His holy name and Krishna bhakti.

Choose the Destination That Matters Most

Thus, *the object of our worship decides our final destination.* Just as no wise traveller boards a random train hoping to reach a specific city, no wise seeker worships just anyone expecting the highest truth.

Krishna alone can grant liberation, eternal life, and boundless bliss in His spiritual realm. Others may give temporary results, but He alone gives the eternal gift of Himself.

Still, Krishna is not a dictator. He lovingly allows each soul to grow at their own pace. And the beauty is—*even sincere worship of others, if done with pure heart and selflessness, eventually leads to Him*, guided by the deity one worships. That's because He is the ultimate source and goal of all worship.

So let us not settle for pebbles when diamonds are being offered.

Let us follow in the footsteps of the wise Brahmana, who threw away the touchstone to receive the real treasure—Krishna's holy names and love.

In the end, it is not just worship that matters. It is *whom* we worship.

32

A Leaf, A Fruit, A Heart

What if you were told that the Supreme Lord—master of all worlds, possessor of endless opulence—can be completely won over with nothing more than a leaf, a flower, a fruit or a little water? Would you believe it? Let us explore.

The Only Requirement: A Loving Heart

In a world where people chase validation through wealth, status and grandeur, it sounds almost unbelievable that God is pleased not by gold or rituals, but by the sincerity of the heart. Yet this is exactly what Krishna declares in the Bhagavad Gita (9.26):

patraṁ puṣpaṁ phalaṁ toyaṁ
yo me bhaktyā prayacchati

tad ahaṁ bhakty-upahṛtam
aśnāmi prayatātmanaḥ

'If one offers Me with love and devotion a leaf, a flower, a fruit or water, I will accept it.'

Not palaces, not diamonds, not elaborate ceremonies—but a simple offering made with love. A Tulsi leaf becomes more valuable than all the riches of the world—if offered with devotion. A child's broken grains are more delightful than a king's feast—if given in love.

This is the staggering simplicity of Krishna consciousness. It levels every playing field and opens the doors of divine love to everyone—rich or poor, educated or unlettered, young or old.

You don't need a perfect life to approach Krishna. You only need a loving heart.

Let us enter the beauty of this path, where the currency of the soul is devotion, and even the humblest act of love becomes a gateway to eternity.

A Beautiful Path

The opportunity to connect with Krishna and thus create one's good fortune is open to everyone. And it is a privilege and an opportunity that no one should ignore. Why would anyone deny themselves the chance to experience divine love, eternal bliss and perfect knowledge through such a simple and profound method?

Krishna desires only love and devotion—nothing else. He joyfully accepts even the smallest offering from a sincere devotee. Gautamiya Tantra offers a beautiful verse to substantiate this point:

tulasī-dala-mātreṇa
jalasya culukena vā
vikrīṇīte svam ātmānaṁ
bhaktebhyo bhakta-vatsalaḥ

'Śrī Krishna, who is very affectionate toward His devotees, sells Himself to a devotee who offers Him merely a tulsī leaf and a palmful of water.'

Is it so difficult? Even if we cannot offer anything else, at least we can start offering some water and Tulsi leaves at His lotus feet. This simple act is enough to please Krishna. In other words, the simplest of offerings attracts the Supreme Grace of Krishna into our lives, which creates our good fortune.

We Gain a Thousand Times

Krishna is the master of all opulence, and when He is pleased with our devotional acts, He gives so much in return that we will not be able to handle with our two hands; even ten hands wouldn't be enough.

But from someone who lacks devotion, no grand sacrifice or opulent gift will move Him. Being self-sufficient, He has no need for anything, yet He cherishes the love His devotees offer Him.

Duryodhana served Krishna with the nicest of food offerings in vessels made of pure gold and silver, but Krishna did not accept any. However, He lovingly ate the banana peels from the hands of Vidurani (a simple devotee and wife of Vidura). Vidurani was so excited to see Krishna that she ended up feeding the banana peels and throwing the bananas away instead of doing it the other way around. But Krishna happily ate that, too, as He, in truth, was tasting her devotion. Without love and devotion, Krishna does not accept any offering of wealth, food or money.

Life's Supreme Mission

The true essence of life is to develop such pure love for the Lord. The importance of bhakti, or loving devotional service, is emphasized time and again in sacred teachings, making it clear that bhakti alone is the way to truly connect with Krishna. One's social status, intellect, wealth or scholarly achievements do not impress Him. Without bhakti, nothing else can bring us closer to Him.

Ultimately, the path to divine fulfilment is not about how much we have or what we achieve in this world—it is about the depth of our devotion and love for

Krishna (God). This is the true key to a life of spiritual joy, purpose and liberation. This is the ultimate goal of human life.

Many times, people ask how we can engage our children in bhakti. Here is the simplest of starts: begin offering these simple things and make them do the same as well. It does not take much time and energy, and it is also the most powerful form of act of devotion, which will fetch them unlimited divine grace.

Anything offered with devotion is accepted by Krishna and if Krishna accepts even a single offering of ours, our human life is a success.

The Fruit Seller's Devotion

In Mathura, a fruit seller often heard travellers speak of a beautiful child named Krishna, the son of Nanda and Yashoda in Gokul. Yearning to see Him, she filled her basket with fruits and set off for Nanda Bhavan.

As she called out, 'Fruits for sale!' time and again, she hoped to catch a glimpse of Krishna. But He was always asleep, playing or in His mother's lap. Determined, she vowed not to leave until she saw Him.

Her calls soon turned into a chant: 'Govinda, Dāmodara, Mādhava!' unknowingly engaging in kirtan, the easiest way to attract Krishna.

Exhausted, she sat near Nanda Bhavan. At noon, Krishna, wearing only a gold chain with tinkling bells, appeared with tiny hands full of grains. As He walked toward her, the grains slipped through His fingers, yet He eagerly gazed at the sweet fruits.

Enchanted, the fruit seller asked Krishna to call her 'Mother' in exchange for the fruits. With childlike innocence, Krishna complied, and she joyfully gave Him as many as He could carry. Yashoda distributed the fruits among the Gopis, but miraculously, the supply never ran out.

Overwhelmed, the fruit seller sat in blissful trance. When she finally left for Mathura, she found her basket overflowing with jewels. But she thought, 'Now that I have got these jewels, I will no longer be required to sell fruits. Does that mean I will no longer be able to see Krishna?'

Unattached, she cast them into the River Yamuna, her heart now filled with Krishna's love. She transcended material desires and attained Goloka Vrindavan, where she would serve Krishna eternally.

He Is Ready. But Are We?

Thus, in a world obsessed with grand gestures and superficial achievements, Krishna reminds us of a far more intimate truth: He does not need our riches—He desires our hearts. What moves Him is not the size of our offering but the sincerity behind it. A Tulsi leaf, a palmful of water, a single grain—when offered with love—becomes more precious than mountains of gold.

The Supreme Lord is won over by the devotion of the simplest soul.

Whether you are a child with tiny hands full of falling grains, or a poor fruit seller chanting in desperation, if your heart is calling for Him, Krishna will come running. He came for the banana peels of Vidurani. He came for the broken grains of the fruit seller. And He is ready to come for us too.

But the question is—will we call out to Him with that same eagerness and love?

Let us not wait till life exhausts us. Let us begin today—with something simple, sincere, and sweet. A Tulsi leaf. A little water. A heartfelt "Hare Krishna." That's all it takes to attract the All-Attractive. Because in the end, the true wealth of life is not what we earn, but whom we serve.

And if we serve Krishna with love, we have already achieved the highest success.

33

Saints with Scars

How Krishna Loves the Imperfect

There is always hope for everyone, even for the most fallen. Loving those who embody only virtues is relatively easy—such ideal souls naturally inspire us, kindling within us the aspiration to refine ourselves. Their purity serves as a guiding light, drawing us toward our highest potential. Yet, in this world, truly ideal people are rare. Even among sincere spiritual seekers, perfection remains a work in progress.

The Myth of the Ideal Circle

The reality is that we are surrounded by individuals—just like ourselves—who possess both virtues and vices. If we reserve our love and service for a social circle of only ideal people, then we will stay waiting for the rest of eternity; such a circle doesn't exist in this world.

If somehow, we find such a circle, would we ourselves qualify for entry? Imperfect as we are, we too would stand at its threshold, unworthy of inclusion. The truth is, spiritual growth happens not in a utopia of perfection, but in the embrace of imperfect hearts striving together toward the divine.

Krishna's Love for the Flawed

Krishna Himself doesn't limit his love to perfect people—He embraces everyone, flaws and all. His love is so boundless that He repeatedly descends from the spiritual world into this imperfect material realm, just to offer us the ultimate gift: eternal love.

As the Bhagavad Gita (4.10) states:

vīta-rāga-bhaya-krodhā
man-mayā mām upāśritāḥ
bahavo jñāna-tapasā
pūtā mad-bhāvam āgatāḥ

'Being free from attachment, fear and anger, fully absorbed in Me and taking refuge in Me, many persons in the past became purified by knowledge and asceticism and thus, attained My divine love.'

Sometimes, we may see a person practising Krishna bhakti make a serious mistake—something considered socially or even politically unacceptable. Past conditionings are very strong. However, this does not disqualify them from spiritual progress.

The Shrimad Bhagavatam (11.5.42) explains that if a devotee stumbles but remains wholeheartedly engaged in serving the Supreme Lord, then Krishna, who resides in their heart, purifies them and forgives their shortcomings.

> *sva-pāda-mūlam bhajataḥ priyasya*
> *tyaktānya-bhāvasya hariḥ pareśaḥ*
> *vikarma yac cotpatitaṁ kathañcid*
> *dhunoti sarvaṁ hṛdi sanniviṣṭaḥ*

> 'One who has thus given up all other engagements and has taken full shelter at the lotus feet of Hari, the Supreme Personality of Godhead, is very dear to the Lord. Indeed, if such a surrendered soul accidentally commits some sinful activity, the Supreme Personality of Godhead, who is seated within everyone's heart, immediately takes away the reaction to such sin.'

His Mercy Is Greater Than Our Mistakes

The material world is full of distractions, and even a dedicated seeker can sometimes falter. However, the power of Krishna bhakti is so great that any occasional misstep is automatically corrected. This means that the process of devotional service is always victorious.

No one should criticize or look down upon a sincere practitioner for an accidental mistake.

As Krishna emphatically declares in the Bhagavad Gita (9.30):

> *api cet su-durācāro*
> *bhajate mām ananya-bhāk*
> *sādhur eva sa mantavyaḥ*
> *samyag vyavasito hi saḥ*

> 'Even if one commits the most abominable action, if they are engaged in My devotional service with determination, they must be considered saintly, because they are properly situated in their resolve.'

The phrase ***sādhur eva*** ('he is saintly') is particularly emphatic. It serves as a warning not to judge a devotee based on an accidental downfall. The word ***mantavyaḥ*** ('must be considered') is even stronger—it is an order from the Supreme Lord.

Krishna has promised in the Bhagavad Gita (9.31):

> *kṣipraṁ bhavati dharmātmā*
> *śaśvac-chāntiṁ nigacchati*
> *kaunteya pratijānīhi*
> *na me bhaktaḥ praṇaśyati*

> 'He quickly becomes righteous and attains lasting peace. O son of Kunti, declare it boldly that My devotee never perishes.'

Do Not Judge

Anyone who disregards this instruction and criticizes a devotee for their past mistakes is actually opposing the will of Krishna.

The only real qualification of a devotee is their unwavering dedication to Krishna. If they sincerely chant the holy names of the Lord:

Hare Krishna, Hare Krishna, Krishna Krishna, Hare Hare/Hare Rama, Hare Rama, Ram Rama, Hare Hare

. . . then they should be considered to be on the elevated platform, even if they temporarily slip due to past conditioning.

The Nrisimha Purana beautifully illustrates this with the following verse:

bhagavati ca harāv ananya-cetā
bhṛśa-malino 'pi virājate manuṣyaḥ
na hi śaśa-kaluṣa-cchabiḥ kadācit
timira-parābhavatām upaiti candraḥ

'Even if a person fully engaged in the devotional service of Lord Hari sometimes appears impure, they still shine brightly, just like the moon. The moon may have dark spots, but these do not stop it from illuminating the night.'

Similarly, a devotee's temporary misstep does not define their spiritual progress.

Don't Take it For Granted

However, this should never be misinterpreted as permission to act irresponsibly. This verse applies only to accidental mistakes caused by material influences. Devotional service, in essence, is a battle against illusion (maya), and as long as one isn't completely spiritually strong, they may occasionally stumble. But once they reach spiritual maturity, such downfalls will no longer happen.

No one should misuse this teaching to justify bad behaviour while claiming to be a devotee. If someone does not show real improvement in character through their spiritual practice, then it is clear that they have not yet reached a high level of devotion. True bhakti is about sincerity, not excuses.

And, just like Krishna, His pure devotees also extend their love to all, guiding others to rediscover their lost connection with Him. By learning how to love even imperfect people—wisely and selflessly—we align ourselves with Krishna's mission. In doing so, we receive His mercy and the grace of His devotees, propelling us faster toward the world of eternal love.

In this imperfect world, it is not perfection that Krishna seeks—it is sincerity. He is not impressed by spotless records or flawless behaviour, but by the relentless sincerity of a heart that keeps turning toward Him despite its struggles. Just as the moon shines despite its spots, a devotee continues to radiate light even if marred by moments of darkness.

34

Krishna

The Origin

Imagine someone wanting to become a doctor but refusing to study medical textbooks or learn from certified professors—instead, they rely on gossip, opinions and social media posts. Would you trust them with your life?

Now ask yourself: why do we treat the subject of God—the most important truth of all—with less seriousness?

Get Educated from the Right Source

Just as knowledge of medicine comes from medical books and qualified doctors, knowledge of God must come from the scriptures and the realized saints who have mastered them.

Anyone who truly studies the Vedas and follows the path of great authorities like Lord Chaitanya, Shri Madhvacharya, Shri Vallabhacharya and Vyasadeva reaches one undeniable conclusion: Krishna is the Supreme Source—of all creation, of all knowledge, of all love.

And once we realize that, there is no confusion left. We no longer chase every loud opinion or trendy philosophy. We anchor ourselves in truth—and dedicate our life to devote ourselves to Krishna. Because in matters of God, guesswork is dangerous. Only guidance from the genuine experts can take us to the goal.

The Ultimate Proof

If we wish to know a person, the best source of information would be when he himself reveals the truth about himself. Even though various vedic sources confirm that Krishna is the origin of Brahma, Shiva and all other celestial beings, Krishna, personally, also declares in the Bhagavad Gita (10.8):

ahaṁ sarvasya prabhavo
mattaḥ sarvaṁ pravartate
iti matvā bhajante māṁ
budhā bhāva-samanvitāḥ

'I am the source of all spiritual and material worlds. Everything emanates from Me. The wise who perfectly know this engage in My devotional service and worship Me with all their hearts.'

This verse, along with revealing the supreme knowledge about Krishna, also states the result of knowing about Krishna: People who know Him become enlightened and wholeheartedly devoted to Him.

The knowledge of God is not meant to be merely theoretical or informational, it is meant to be profoundly transformational; it should purify our hearts of all vices and increase our faith. If our scriptural hearing, study or following of a certain path does not cause this transformation and does not lead us to engage in His loving devotional service, then our endeavours are absolutely futile.

Lost Children of a Wealthy Man

To appreciate why, consider the metaphor of an orphan boy who happens to gather a piece of information about himself: he is the lost child of a billionaire. That knowledge would spur him into learning how to reconnect with his father and make all efforts to be reunited. If he didn't make any such efforts at all, it could well be argued that he hadn't understood that information. The same applies to our knowledge of God.

To know God means to know that we all are his beloved children. Just as He is eternal and eternally blissful, so too are we meant to be. But when we see

Him merely as a source of fulfilling our worldly desires, or for freeing us from worldly problems, then we don't really know Him.

Those who know God devote themselves to him; those who know Krishna are thus left with no option except to become devoted to Him. That doesn't mean they are forced against their will; it just means that the intellectual persuasiveness of knowledge of God's position makes any other course of action un-intellectual or even anti-intellectual. Thus, this Gita verse inverts the charge sometimes levelled against bhakti; it is for the non-intellectual or sentimental. Such devotion may be practiced by those who know just a little about God, but those who know Him truly are a different category indeed.

The Vedic Evidence

The Atharva Veda (Gopāla-tāpanī Upaniṣad 1.24) states:

> *yo brahmāṇaṁ vidadhāti pūrvaṁ yo vai vedāṁś ca gāpayati sma Krishnaḥ*
>
> 'It was Krishna who, in the beginning, instructed Brahmā in Vedic knowledge and who disseminated that knowledge in the past.'

The Narayana Upanishad (1) declares:

atha puruṣo ha vai nārāyaṇo 'kāmayata prajāḥ sṛjeyeti

'The Supreme Personality, Narayana, desired to create living beings.'

It further states:

nārāyaṇād brahmā jāyate, nārāyaṇād prajāpatiḥ prajāyate, nārāyaṇād indro jāyate, nārāyaṇād aṣṭau vasavo jāyante, nārāyaṇād ekādaśa rudrā jāyante, nārāyaṇād dvādaśādityāḥ

'From Narayana, Brahma is born, from Narayana come the patriarchs, Indra, the eight Vasus, the eleven Rudras, and the twelve Adityas.'

This confirms that Narayaṇa, an expansion of Krishna, is the source of all creation.

The Narayana Upaniṣad (4) further declares:

brahmaṇyo devakī-putraḥ

'The son of Devaki, Krishna, is the Supreme Lord.'

The Mahā Upaniṣad (1.2) describes the state before creation:

eko vai nārāyaṇa āsīn na brahmā neśāno nāpo nāgni-somau neme dyāv-āpṛthivī na nakṣatrāṇi na sūryaḥ

'In the beginning, only Narayaṇa existed. There was no Brahma, no Shiva, no water, no fire, no moon, no sky, no stars, and no sun.'

The same Upaniṣad also states that Lord Shiva was born from the forehead of the Supreme Lord. This establishes that the creator of Brahma and Shiva is the Supreme Being, who alone is worthy of worship.

Krishna Himself confirms in the Mahabharata (Moksha-dharma 340.10–11):

prajāpatiṁ ca rudraṁ cāpy
aham eva sṛjāmi vai
tau hi māṁ na vijānīto
mama māyā-vimohitau

'I create the patriarchs, Shiva and others, yet they do not recognize that I am their source because they are bewildered by My illusory energy.'

Similarly, the Varaha Purana (24.29–30) states:

nārāyaṇaḥ paro devas
tasmāj jātaś caturmukhaḥ
tasmād rudro 'bhavad devaḥ
sa ca sarva-jñatāṁ gataḥ

'Narayana is the Supreme God. From Him, Brahma was born, and from Brahmā came Śiva.'

Further, He declares in the Bhagavad Gita (14.4):

sarva-yoniṣu kaunteya
mūrtayaḥ sambhavanti yāḥ
tāsāṁ brahma mahad yonir
ahaṁ bīja-pradaḥ pitā

'It should be understood that all species of life, O son of Kunti (Arjuna), are made possible by birth in this material nature, and that I am the seed-giving father.'

In the Noise of Opinions, Let the Gita Speak

A true seeker should not be swayed by misleading interpretations. In a world full of opinions, half-truths and spiritual shortcuts, clarity is rare—and priceless. But for one who seeks the truth from the right sources—the Vedas, the Bhagavad Gita and the great acharyas—there is no room left for doubt: Krishna is the Supreme Truth, the origin of all, the object of all worship and the ultimate shelter of the soul.

He has declared it. The scriptures confirm it. The saints have lived it. Now, the only question that remains is—will we accept it?

35

From Craving to Celebrating

We get attracted by opulence: beauty, knowledge, strength, wealth, fame and renunciation. Whenever we see something beautiful, brilliant or extraordinary, our natural response is admiration. But often, admiration comes with an unwanted side effect—desire. When someone else has something that we don't, we may feel a craving to possess it. And if we can't, that craving can turn into frustration, dissatisfaction or even resentment.

But the hard truth is that we can't own everything we admire. Our resources—whether wealth, talent or beauty—are limited. Even the wealthiest person in the world doesn't have everything. Someone will always be smarter, more talented or more attractive. And even if we somehow acquire everything we ever wanted, there would still be things beyond our grasp—like someone else's genius, charisma or natural grace. So, how do we free ourselves from the cycle of wanting and feeling unfulfilled?

Krishna's Spark: The Source of All Beauty

The Bhagavad Gita offers a powerful shift in perspective—one that allows us to admire without the burden of wanting to acquire. Krishna explains:

yad yad vibhūtimat sattvaṁ
śrīmad ūrjitam eva vā
tat tad evāvagaccha tvaṁ
mama tejo-'ṁśa-sambhavam

Bhagavad Gita (10.41)

> 'Whatever is beautiful, glorious or powerful in this world, know that it springs from just a spark of My splendour.'

Everything that captivates us—whether it's beauty, intelligence, strength or charm—is just a tiny fragment of Krishna's infinite attractiveness and opulence.

When we practice Bhakti Yoga and make Krishna the center of our lives, we begin to experience joy in remembering Him as the ultimate source of all that is wonderful. Instead of feeling envious or lacking, we feel connected to an unlimited reservoir of beauty and brilliance. As we chant Krishna's holy names on a daily basis and hear the wisdom of the scriptures from the devotees of the Lord, we start seeing things in relation to Krishna. We start seeing the futility of focusing on what others have and begin to focus on the blessings bestowed upon us. Whatever we focus upon expands in our life.

Shift from Possessing to Praising

With this mindset, admiration turns into celebration. When we see something amazing, we shouldn't think, 'Why don't I have that?' Instead, we must think, 'Wow, this reminds me of Krishna!' and how Krishna's supreme beauty is manifesting through this person—that thought itself becomes a source of happiness.

No one is the real owner except the Supreme Lord. We come into this world with nothing, and we go back with nothing. So what shall we gain by becoming attached or possessing anything of this world when we do not even belong here?

We are souls, spiritual beings meant to rejoice in eternal love with Krishna, but our conditionings have trapped our consciousness at the material level, thereby making spiritual happiness inaccessible.

The Misfit of Spirit and Matter

No amount of material fulfilment can give us real happiness since we are spiritual by nature, parts and parcels of God. A spiritual being trying to be satisfied by matter is not only an incompatible situation, but also an impossible one.

We should simply focus on our eternal constitutional position and learn of Krishna's beauty and kindness. As soon as the mind becomes focused on the Lord, worldly hankerings disappear.

With this wisdom, which comes as we advance in spiritual life and association with saintly devotees of the Lord, we stop seeing things merely in relation to their temporary owners and start seeing them in connection with their eternal source. The more we do this, the more we become free from the unnecessary hankerings and lamentation as the remembrance of Krishna purifies the heart.

This is the secret to feeling abundant, no matter what we have. Instead of being weighed down by cravings, we feel uplifted by appreciation. And in that space of gratitude, we find a joy that no material possession can ever provide because happiness, success and contentment in life are not dependent on acquisitions and positions, but on our deeper connection with Krishna. A beautiful incident from Alexander's life illustrates this point.

Alexander, the World Conqueror, Conquered

In India, Alexander the Great encountered the one force he could not conquer—the yogis. Greek historians, who accompanied the fierce commander, recorded their astonishing encounter with these enigmatic sages.

Deep in the woods, Alexander's soldiers came across a Brahmana sage, Dandamis, lying on a bed of leaves. Intrigued by the famed wisdom of India's holy men, Alexander sent him a message:

'Alexander, Son of God and Lord of the Earth, summons you to his presence. If you come, you will be richly rewarded. If you refuse, you will die.'

Dandamis remained unimpressed. He sent back a reply:

'There is only one true King—the One who created light and life. He alone do I obey, and He abhors war.'

The sage continued, 'How can Alexander claim to be the King of the Earth when he himself is subject to the King of Death? And what can he offer me when my mother, the Earth, already provides everything I need? I have no possessions to protect, so I sleep peacefully at night. Alexander may destroy my body, but he cannot touch my soul.'

'Tell your King that at the time of death, each of us must account for our actions. Ask him—how will he justify the suffering of those he has slaughtered and oppressed? Your King may tempt those who crave gold. He may terrify those who fear death. But we Brahmins desire neither. Go and tell Alexander: he has nothing I seek, and so I will not see him.'

When Alexander's men returned with the sage's response, the mighty conqueror listened in silence.

Finally, he admitted that he, who had vanquished empires, had been humbled by a single, naked old man.

Three Last Wishes!

As a result of this encounter, Alexander seemed to have absorbed some wisdom which was evident when he was leaving his body.

After conquering many kingdoms, as he charted a return home, he fell sick on the way and life took him to his deathbed. The mighty conqueror lay prostrate and pale, helplessly waiting to breathe his last.

He called his generals and said, 'I will depart from this world soon. I have three wishes, please fulfil them without fail.' With tears flowing down their cheeks, the generals agreed to abide by their king's last wishes.

'My first desire,' said Alexander, 'is that my physicians alone must carry my coffin.'

After a pause, he continued, 'Secondly, I desire that when my coffin is being carried to the grave, the path leading to the graveyard be strewn with gold, silver and precious stones that I have collected in my treasury.'

The king felt exhausted after saying this. He took a minute's rest and continued,

'My third and last wish is that both my hands be kept dangling out of my coffin.'

Alexander's favourite general kissed his hand and pressed them to his heart. 'O king, we assure you that your wishes will all be fulfilled. But tell us why you make such strange wishes.'

At this, Alexander took a deep breath and said, 'I would like the world to know of the three lessons I have just learned. I want my physicians to carry my coffin because people should realize that no doctor can really cure anybody. They are powerless and cannot save a person from the clutches of death. So let not people take life for granted.'

'The second wish of strewing gold, silver and other riches on the way to the graveyard is to tell people that not even a fraction of gold will come with me. I spent all my life earning riches but cannot take anything with me. Let people realize that it is a sheer waste of time to chase wealth.'

'And about my third wish of having my hands dangling out of the coffin, I want people to know that I came empty-handed into this world and empty-handed it is that I go out of this world.'

With these words, the king closed his eyes. Soon, he let death conquer him and breathed his last.

The yogi humbled Alexander, not with armies, but with truth. And Alexander's death humbled the world, reminding us that everything we chase eventually slips through our fingers.

Let us not wait till our final breath to awaken. Let us remember now: True wealth is not in what we collect, but in whom we connect with. Connect with Krishna—and feel fulfilled, forever.

This is what human life's real purpose is: to reduce our material aspirations, not to expand them. We must simply focus on our needs rather than our wants. Wants will have no end. Work for as much as we need and use the rest of the energy to cultivate spiritual wisdom, which gives birth to the essential virtue of satisfaction.

36

Spiritual Wi-Fi

Never Lose Signal with Krishna

What happens when a phone loses signal? You can't call, message or access anything. It becomes a lifeless device in your hand. Now imagine a soul disconnected from Krishna—the Supreme Source of everything. That's how most people live today: constantly active but spiritually offline.

The Bhagavad Gita is a book for such disconnected souls. Its mission? To plug us back into the divine network—to help us reconnect with Krishna, wherever we are, whoever we are and however broken or busy we may feel. That's why it's called a Yoga Shastra—a manual on divine connection. Yoga means 'to connect' with the Supreme.

The result of it? We will attain the highest destination as promised by Krishna in the Bhagavad Gita (11.55), a verse that is considered to be the essence of the Gita:

The Destination is Divine

What is the result of reconnecting with Krishna? It is not just peace of mind or moral improvement. It is the highest destination—eternal life in Krishna's personal abode.

As Krishna promises in the Bhagavad Gita (11.55), a verse considered the very essence of the Gita:

mat-karma-kṛn mat-paramo
mad-bhaktaḥ saṅga-varjitaḥ
nirvairaḥ sarva-bhūteṣu
yaḥ sa mām eti pāṇḍava

> 'My dear Arjuna, he who engages in My pure devotional service, free from the contaminations of fruitive activities (acts performed with selfish motive)and mental speculation, he who works for Me, who makes Me the supreme goal of his life, and who is friendly to every living being—he certainly comes to Me.'

Connection Begins with Seva (Service)

But how do we connect with Krishna? The answer is simple: Through loving service. This service can begin from exactly where we are, with what we already have.

We often think of work as a way to earn, achieve, and succeed. But what if work itself could become an act of worship?

Śrī Rūpa Goswami, a prominent Vaishnava acharya, gives us the mindset in *Bhakti-rasāmṛta-sindhu* (1.2.255):

anāsaktasya viṣayān
yathārham upayuñjataḥ
nirbandhaḥ Krishna-sambandhe
yuktaṁ vairāgyam ucyate

'True renunciation is not rejecting the world, but using everything in connection with Krishna.'

Don't quit your job—redefine it. Work not for your ego, but for Krishna's pleasure. Whether you're running a business, coding, painting, teaching or parenting—offer it to Him. This is called Krishna-karma—work done for Krishna.

Intent Is Everything

It's not what you do that matters most, but why and for whom you do it.

When you see Krishna as the true owner of your work, your business, your home, your talents—your life transforms. Ambition doesn't disappear—it gets divinely redirected. You start asking: What will please Krishna most?

That's when your work becomes more than duty—it becomes a bridge to eternity.

Opportunities Are Everywhere

- Can't build a temple? Clean the temple.
- Don't have wealth? Grow Tulsi or flowers to offer.
- Don't have land? Offer a leaf, a flower, fruit or water—with love. Even the poorest person can serve Krishna meaningfully.

Krishna says in the Gita (9.26):

> *Patraṁ puṣpaṁ phalaṁ toyam*

> 'If one offers Me a leaf, a flower, fruit or water with devotion, I accept it.'

This includes the Tulsi leaf, which Krishna holds especially dear.

Guard Your Association, Nourish Your Soul

Just as we protect our health by choosing what we consume, we must protect our consciousness by choosing our company.

- Keep extremely minimal association with those who lack faith and disrespect the path.
- Seek the company of devotees, those who help you remember Him.
- Daily, chant His holy names, read the Bhagavad Gita and Srimad Bhagavatam, and worship His deity form.

These are not burdens—they are lifelines. They reconnect us to the source of our existence.

Serve Krishna by Serving Souls

To love Krishna is also to love His children. Help others rise higher. Uplift their consciousness. Relieve their distress. And the best way to do that? Help them reconnect with Krishna.

This is the greatest charity. This is Krishna-karma.

When we live in this way—serving Krishna with whatever we have, wherever we are—our life becomes successful. Not just materially, but eternally.

This is the ultimate promise of Krishna in the Gita:

'He who does this certainly comes to Me.'

You don't need to be perfect to begin. You just need to begin. You don't need to have everything. You just need to offer what you do have—with love.

Disconnection from Krishna is the root of all suffering. Connection with Krishna is the root of all fulfilment. The Bhagavad Gita is Krishna's personal call to us: 'Come back. I'm waiting.' Let's not ignore that divine call. Let's answer it—by dedicating our work, our time, our energy and our heart to Him.

Because the ultimate success in life is not about how much we gained in the world . . . but whether we found our way back to Krishna.

So don't wait. Start serving. Start connecting. Not someday—today. Because reconnection with Krishna is not just the purpose of life— it is life.

37

Form or Formless?

A million-dollar question that has intrigued the minds of countless people over the history of mankind: Does God have a form or is He formless? Who can answer this question better than God Himself? Let us explore this.

Limiting God Is the Real Limitation

God means a complete and a perfect personality with no room for any imperfection. If we say He has a form and no formless aspect, then we are limiting Him. If He is God, the all-powerful, why can't He have a formless aspect also? He could be anything that He wishes to. And saying He is formless and cannot have a form is also restricting Him. So, to resolve the issue, we must refer to the scriptures, as the knowledge about God must come from them and not from social media, the opinion of the majority or our own limited perception.

Three Levels of Realization

The Shrimad Bhagavatam (1.2.12) answers:

> *vadanti tat tattva-vidas*
> *tattvaṁ yaj jñānam advayam*
> *brahmeti paramātmeti*
> *bhagavān iti śabdyate*
>
> 'Learned transcendentalists who know the Absolute Truth (God) call this non-dual substance Brahman, Paramatma or Bhagwan.'

This means that God has a form, a formless aspect and something in between also. That makes Him complete and perfect, not lacking in anything.

At the lowest level is the Brahman or the formless aspect, which people address as Brahmajyoti (the blue light). Higher than this is the localized feature or Paramatma (the four-handed Viṣṇu form) situated in everyone's heart and upon which all the yogis meditate. And the highest feature is Bhagwan or the personal feature of the Lord, where we know him as a full person with six luxuries, namely wealth, beauty, knowledge, strength, fame and renunciation.

Let us understand this with the help of an analogy of the sunlight, the sun (globe) and the Sun God. The sunlight aspect represents the Brahman feature or the impersonal feature of the sun. Study of sunlight is not the complete study of the sun. It is the preliminary one. When we go closer, we find that there is a sun globe from where this light emanates, and that is like the Paramatma feature. This is slightly advanced study, but when we enter the sun globe, we see that there is a person, Surya Dev who is controlling the affairs of the sun—and that is like the Bhagwan feature of the Lord. He, in his form, is making things happen for the sun to shine.

Just like sunlight is emitting from the sun and it's not the other way around, the formless aspect of God originated from the form and not otherwise, as some people say.

What Does Krishna Himself Say?

To further understand which aspect of God is superior, let us refer to the Bhagavad Gita (12.1), where Arjuna asks Krishna, 'Some worship your formless aspect and some engage in the devotional service of your personal form, which among the two are considered to be superior?'

arjuna uvāca
evaṁ satata-yuktā ye

bhaktās tvāṁ paryupāsate
ye cāpy akṣaram avyaktaṁ
teṣāṁ ke yoga-vittamāḥ

'Arjuna enquired: Which are considered to be more perfect, those who are always properly engaged in Your devotional service or those who worship the impersonal Brahman, the formless?'

Krishna settles the dispute once and for all, and answers in the next verse, Bhagavad Gita (12.2):

śrī-bhagavān uvāca
mayy āveśya mano ye māṁ
nitya-yuktā upāsate
śraddhayā parayopetās
te me yukta-tamā matāḥ

'The Supreme Lord said: Those who fix their minds on My personal form and are always engaged in worshiping Me with great and transcendental faith are considered by Me to be most perfect.'

He further says in Bhagavad Gita (12.5):

kleśo 'dhika-taras teṣām
avyaktāsakta-cetasām
avyaktā hi gatir duḥkhaṁ
dehavadbhir avāpyate

> 'For those whose minds are attached to the unmanifested, impersonal feature of the Supreme, advancement is very troublesome. To make progress in that discipline is always difficult for those who are embodied.'

We have a body and are used to interacting with forms. Thus, it is extremely difficult to connect with the formless aspect.

Lord Brahma, the first created being in the Universe, also clarifies in Brahma Samhita (5.40):

> *yasya prabhā prabhavato jagad-aṇḍa-koṭi-*
> *koṭiṣv aśeṣa-vasudhādi vibhūti-bhinnam*
> *tad brahma niṣkalam anantam aśeṣa-bhūtaṁ*
> *govindam ādi-puruṣaṁ tam ahaṁ bhajāmi*

> 'I worship Govinda, the primeval Lord, whose radiance is the source of the formless Brahman mentioned in the Upanishads, being differentiated from the infinity of glories of the mundane universe and appears as the indivisible, infinite, limitless truth.'

Thus, it is clear that the Supreme Lord has a form, worship of the form is superior and that form is the source of the formless aspect—just like a bulb is the cause behind the light and not the other way around.

Why Do Some Scriptures Say God Is Formless?

Now, what about certain scriptures that talk about the formless aspect and address God as *nirakar* and *nirgun*?

Well, we must understand that among the scriptures also there is a hierarchy of understanding, and each scripture is catering to a particular category of people in society, who are at different levels of evolution. Among all, the Bhagavad Gita and Shrimad Bhagavatam are at the top and give complete knowledge about God. Other scriptures touch upon some preliminary understanding with the ultimate goal of guiding devotees towards the ultimate understanding. They bring us to a certain level and then we are expected to advance and not remain stuck only with the preliminary knowledge.

When the scriptures say 'nirakar' or without form, this is addressing those people who, due to a narrow understanding, think that God also has a form like theirs and thus try to impose their own consciousness on Him and bring Him down to a mundane or ordinary platform. Thus, to silence such people and save them from such ignorant thinking, scriptures say, He is 'nirakar' Brahman or formless. Immediately, their entire philosophy changes and helps develop reverence towards God.

So, nirakar means that the Lord does not have a mundane form like ours, but He does have a spiritual form.

Again, quoting from the Brahma Samhita (5.1):

sac-cid-ānanda-vigrahaḥ

'Vigrahah' means 'form'.

'Lord Brahma, who is the first created being within the universe and thus knows more than everyone else, explains that the Lord has a form, a divine form that is full of eternity, knowledge and bliss.' (Satchidananda)

When some scriptures use 'nirgun', it does not mean that the Lord had no qualities. It simply means that He has no mundane qualities like us. And there are three gunas (goodness, passion and ignorance) that bind all of us and predominate the material world. But God is beyond them as He is supremely independent and thus cannot be bound by anything. Hence, He is known as nirgun.

A Logical Understanding

Imagine this: Every person you have ever known—your father, his father, his ancestors—all had a form. From time immemorial, human beings have existed in a tangible, visible form. So, when we claim that the Supreme Father, the origin of everything, has no form, does that really make sense? If we, as tiny fragments of His creation, possess form and personality, why would He, the source of all existence, be formless and impersonal?

If we look at the pastimes of the Divine, we see that He has always acted through a form. Every divine **leela** (**pastime**) described in the scriptures—be it Krishna lifting Govardhan Hill, Ram defeating Ravana, or Narasimha protecting Prahalad—was performed in a **personal, visible form.** Every word of wisdom spoken by Him—whether in the Bhagavad Gita, the Vedas or the Upanishads—was spoken by a divine personality.

If form was irrelevant, why would the scriptures emphasize it so much?

Some argue that God is formless, but what they fail to understand is that God is both formless and with form. He is formless in the sense that He is not bound by material limitations like us. Yet, He possesses a transcendental form, beyond birth, decay, or death. This is why the Bhagavad Gita (4.6) states:

ajo 'pi sann avyayātmā bhūtānām īśvaro 'pi san

'Although I am unborn and My transcendental body never deteriorates, and although I am the Lord of all living entities, by My internal energy I still appear in every millennium in My original transcendental form.'

Can We Love a Formless God?

If God were truly impersonal, how would love for Him even be possible? Relationships are built with people, not with abstract energy. The essence of bhakti (devotion) is a personal connection—loving Him, serving Him and seeing Him as the ultimate beloved. Just as we form relationships with our friends, family and mentors, we are meant to form a deep, loving relationship with Krishna, the Supreme Lord.

So, rather than limiting God by saying He has no form, let's recognize the beauty of His divine, eternal and all-attractive form—the very form that has captivated countless souls for millennia.

Those who claim that God has no form are, perhaps unknowingly, limiting Him.

The real glory of God is that He is beyond limitations. He is both with form and beyond form. His form is not material—it is transcendental. It is beautiful, blissful and eternal.

And most importantly—it is lovable.

When we understand that Krishna is not just the all-pervading energy but a loving, divine person, our hearts naturally open to Him. We stop fearing God as some distant force and start loving Him as our eternal father, mother, friend and beloved.

Let's not settle for a light when we can embrace the source of all light. Let's not remain in awe of the impersonal when we are invited into a personal relationship. Let us approach Krishna—not as a mystery to be debated, but as a person to be loved.

Because when God becomes personal to us—life becomes eternal.

38

Rising Above Our Lower Nature

Why Do We Do What We Do?

Ever wondered why people are so different from each other? Why does one person love the colour pink, while another prefers blue? Why does one person enjoy spicy food while another can't handle even a hint of chilli? Why does one person thrive in a messy room while another can't stand even a little clutter?

Even in the same situation, different people react differently—some stay calm while others get agitated. Some are naturally peaceful, while others are constantly restless. But where does all this come from? Our preferences, personalities and inclinations are shaped by something deep within us.

Personality tests and psychology courses categorize us into different types, highlighting our strengths and weaknesses. But do they ever explain where our personality originates? Why do we like what we like? Why do we instinctively gravitate toward certain things?

We think we are making our own choices but, in reality, something is controlling us. What is that force? The Bhagavad Gita reveals the answer—it is the three gunas (modes of material nature), which literally means 'ropes' that bind us.

The Three Gunas: The Invisible Forces Controlling Us

The Bhagavad Gita (14.5) states:

sattvaṁ rajas tama iti guṇāḥ prakṛti-sambhavāḥ
nibadhnanti mahā-bāho dehe dehinam avyayam

'Material nature consists of three modes—goodness, passion and ignorance. When the eternal living entity comes in contact with nature, O mighty-armed Arjuna, he becomes conditioned by these modes.'

He further says in Bhagavad Gita (17.3) and (17.7):

sattvānurūpā sarvasya
śraddhā bhavati bhārata
śraddhā-mayo 'yaṁ puruṣo
yo yac-chraddhaḥ sa eva saḥ

'O son of Bharata, according to one's existence under the various modes of nature, one evolves a particular kind of faith. The living being is said to be of a particular faith according to the modes he has acquired.'

āhāras tv api sarvasya
tri-vidho bhavati priyaḥ
yajñas tapas tathā dānaṁ
teṣāṁ bhedam imaṁ śṛṇu

'Even the food each person prefers is of three kinds, according to the three modes of material nature. The same is true of sacrifices, austerities and charity.'

Imagine being tied with three ropes—each pulling in a different direction. We are not as independent as we think. The moment that the soul enters this world, it is influenced by the three modes. Every object, activity and thought in this world falls under one of these three categories. The choices we make condition us to one of the gunas. Each guna has a set of qualities associated with it and whichever guna we associate with by making particular choices, we develop corresponding qualities.

1. **Sattva (Goodness):** Brings clarity, knowledge and peace.
2. **Rajas (Passion):** Fuels ambition, desire and restlessness.

3. **Tamas (Ignorance):** Causes laziness, confusion and darkness.

Over time, our repeated actions **create a pattern,** and this pattern becomes our nature. **In our next life, we are born with the same nature, inclinations and desires we cultivated in our past lives.**

Examples of the Three Gunas in Action

Even within the same family, we see different personalities influenced by the three modes. Take the example of **Kumbhakarna, Ravana, and Vibhishana:**

- **Vibhishana (Goodness):** Peaceful, wise and devoted.
- **Ravana (Passion):** Ambitious, driven but blinded by desire.
- **Kumbhakarna (Ignorance):** Addicted to food, sleep and indulgence.

This is why people behave in certain ways and change is so difficult. It's not just a habit—it's a deep-rooted conditioning carried over lifetimes.

How Can We Rise Above These Gunas?

If our nature is so deeply ingrained, is there any way to change? The Bhagavad Gita (14.26) provides the solution:

māṁ ca yo 'vyabhicāreṇa bhakti-yogena sevate
sa guṇān samatītyaitān brahma-bhūyāya kalpate

'One who engages in full devotional service, unfailing in all circumstances, at once transcends the modes of material nature and thus comes to the level of Brahman.'

Krishna is beyond these gunas. Only someone who is free can free others. When we take the shelter of Krishna through Bhakti Yoga (devotional service), we rise above our lower nature.

Transforming Our Nature Through Bhakti

So how do we connect with Krishna and break free from these ropes?

- **Chanting His holy names:** The more we chant, the more we purify our consciousness.
- **Studying the Bhagavad Gita and Shrimad Bhagavatam:** Wisdom elevates our thinking.
- **Visiting the temple and worshipping Krishna:** Strengthens our spiritual connection.
- **Serving devotees and engaging in selfless service:** Helps us develop humility and gratitude.
- **Keeping good company:** The right association can transform us.

Even if we can't fully engage in bhakti, praying to Krishna for help is powerful. We can ask for His mercy—to resist temptations and choose what uplifts us.

Real Change Comes from Within

Many people try to change themselves or others through self-help techniques, but these changes are often temporary because real change is not so easy. The gunas are very strong. We need the higher powers' help to change. A person might try to change by going through some so-called meditation techniques or going through some wellness regimen, but it might just make him feel better and not cause any real transformation. Unless there is a real change from within, all our efforts are useless.

The real test of a person's nature is not in normal situations but in temptations or provoking ones.

The Bhagavad Gita (2.14) says:

mātrā-sparśās tu kaunteya śītoṣṇa-sukha-duḥkha-dāḥ
āgamāpāyino 'nityās tāṁs titikṣasva bhārata

'O son of Kunti, the impermanent appearance of happiness and distress, and their disappearance in due course, are like the appearance and disappearance of winter and summer seasons. They arise from sense perception, and one must learn to tolerate them without being disturbed.'

We may act composed on the outside, but when life squeezes us like a sponge, our true nature comes out. If we want to truly transform, we must go beyond surface-level change and cleanse our hearts through Krishna's grace.

The Power of Association and Superior Guidance

The kind of company we keep shapes our choices. Take the example of Ratnakar, a feared bandit who robbed and murdered people. Yet, just by associating with a saint, he transformed into Valmiki, the revered sage who later wrote the Ramayana.

Similarly, Haridas Thakur was once tested by a prostitute, but his deep devotion transformed not just himself but also the woman who tried to tempt him.

Change is possible—but it requires higher guidance. Just as a child doesn't know the dangers of fire and needs a parent to warn him, we need the wisdom of Guru, God and scripture to make the right choices.

Choices Shape Your Future

Everything we do—the food we eat, the words we speak, the company we keep and the actions we take—strengthens a particular mode within us. We are constantly shaping our future with every decision we make.

The Bhagavad Gita gives us a roadmap to making the best choices, rising above our conditioning, and ultimately attaining spiritual freedom. By aligning ourselves with Krishna and seeking the guidance of enlightened souls, we can break free from our lower nature and become the best versions of ourselves.

So, the next time we find ourselves wondering why we behave in a certain way—or why change feels so hard—we must remember this: it is the past conditioning. But we have the power to transcend, transform and elevate our consciousness—one choice at a time. Our past choices have brought us to the present situation and our present choices will design our future because after all, we are nothing but the products of our own choices. No matter what we have done till now and how strong a conditioning might be, with superior guidance and grace, any change is possible.

39

The Three Gates to Hell

In the journey of self-improvement and spiritual evolution, one must consciously strive to overcome three formidable enemies of the soul: lust, anger and greed. These three vices are the root causes of all other negative tendencies and lead to the degradation of the self. As Lord Krishna teaches in the Bhagavad Gita, overcoming these enemies is essential for inner peace, self-realization and a truly fulfilling life. He deems these three drives self-destructive in Bhagavad Gita (16.21):

tri-vidhaṁ narakasyedaṁ
dvāraṁ nāśanam ātmanaḥ
kāmaḥ krodhas tathā lobhas
tasmād etat trayaṁ tyajet

> 'There are three gates leading to this hell—lust, anger and greed. Every sane man should give these up, for they lead to the degradation of the soul.'

The Dangerous Digital Age

Our devices these days provide us ready access to almost countless stimuli that can trigger lust, anger and greed within us. Just by a click or two, we can see the obscenest images that may drive the lust within us mad or we may see a dizzying array of consumer products that may inflame us with greed, or we can be exposed to biased or bigoted propaganda that can fill us with anger. Thus, because getting infected with these lower emotions is so easy, we are essentially carrying the red zones with us.

What earlier took effort to find now comes chasing after us. The battle for self-control is no longer far away—it's right in our hands, lighting up our screens with constant alerts. If we don't stay alert and protect our mind, these temptations can quietly take over and steal our peace, self-respect and even our deeper goals in life.

Lust: The All-Devouring Enemy of the Soul

Lust (kaam) is not merely a physical desire but an obsessive craving for personal gratification. It blinds a person, distorts their vision and renders them incapable of distinguishing between right and wrong. Krishna, in the third chapter of the Bhagavad Gita, explicitly calls lust 'the eternal enemy of the soul', explaining that it resides within the senses, mind and intelligence, corrupting them completely. He instructs Arjuna—and by extension, all of us—to destroy this formidable enemy through spiritual wisdom and self-discipline.

The example of Ravana in the Ramayana is a cautionary tale of lust's destructive power. Despite having Mandodari, one of the most beautiful and virtuous wives, and countless women serving him, his insatiable desire led him to abduct Mother Sita, the divine consort of Lord Rama. Even when advised against it by his own brother, Kumbhakarna, and his well-wishers, he remained blinded by lust and met his downfall.

Arjuna asks Krishna in the Gita, 'What is it that compels a person to act sinfully, even against their own better judgement?' Krishna replies that it is lust alone. When someone or something obstructs our sense gratification, we see them as an enemy. The best way to control this overpowering force is through spiritual practice. The Vaishnav acharyas explain that meditating on Krishna, especially on His transcendental, playful pastimes with the Gopis as described in the Shrimad Bhagavatam 10th Canto, helps one transcend material lust. Chanting the holy names of Krishna—*Hare Krishna, Hare Krishna, Krishna Krishna, Hare Hare,*

Hare Rama, Hare Rama, Rama Rama, Hare Hare—cleanses the heart, gradually replacing lust with divine love.

Anger: A Moment of Rage, a Lifetime of Regret

Speak when you are angry and you will make the worst speeches of your life. Anger (*krodha*) is one of the most destructive emotions a person can experience. A single moment of uncontrolled anger can ruin relationships, careers and even lives. It is rightly said that 'anger is just one letter short of danger'. History is filled with examples of people who, in a fit of rage, have committed irreversible mistakes—acts of violence, words spoken that left deep wounds, and decisions that led to lifelong regret.

Krishna explains in the Bhagavad Gita that anger arises when desires are frustrated. When we do not get what we want, or someone obstructs our plans, anger flares up and clouds our judgement. An angry person loses the ability to think rationally and ends up causing harm not only to others but also to themselves. The key to overcoming anger is self-awareness and purification of the heart. Just as lust can be cleansed by chanting the holy names of Krishna and hearing His divine pastimes, so too can anger be dissolved through spiritual practice. A heart filled with love and devotion leaves no room for the fire of rage.

Greed: The Insatiable Thirst for More

When lust is fulfilled, it leads to greed (*lobha*). The nature of material enjoyment is such that once a desire is satisfied, another one arises. The more we indulge, the more we crave. We deceive ourselves into believing that acquiring wealth, possessions and power will bring lasting satisfaction, but in reality, it only deepens our dissatisfaction.

Someone has said, 'The world has enough for everyone's need, but not for one man's greed.' The more a person accumulates, the more they desire, and this endless cycle leads to anxiety, competition and suffering. Greed turns a person blind to the needs of others and creates an illusion that happiness is found in material possessions.

The Shrimad Bhagavatam offers a profound lesson through the story of King Bali and Lord Vamana. When Lord Vamana, appearing as a small Brahmana boy, asked for just three steps of land, King Bali was puzzled. He offered him vast kingdoms and wealth, but the Lord replied that a person who is not satisfied with three steps of land will not be satisfied even if they own the entire universe. True satisfaction comes not from external accumulation but from inner contentment.

To counteract greed, one must shift focus from 'what I want' to 'what I truly need'. By cultivating the virtue of satisfaction and engaging in acts of charity, we free ourselves from the clutches of greed. When we learn to share our resources with others, our consciousness elevates, and we experience true fulfilment.

The Path to Purification

Whether it is lust, anger or greed, these vices stem from deep-rooted impurities in the heart. Krishna provides the ultimate solution in the Bhagavad Gita—constant remembrance of Him. By regularly chanting the holy names of Krishna, meditating on His divine form and serving others with a pure heart, we cleanse our inner being. This purification process gradually diminishes the hold of these negative forces and replaces them with divine qualities such as compassion, humility and selflessness.

Thus, if one truly desires to improve their life and elevate their consciousness, they must strive daily to overcome these three great enemies of the soul. Through sincere spiritual practice and persistent prayers, one can break free from their grip and experience the boundless joy of divine love and eternal peace.

40

Scriptures

The Timeless Relevance

In any well-functioning society, laws exist to maintain order and protect its citizens. Just as those who violate legal statutes must face the consequences, individuals who disregard scriptural injunctions inevitably face karmic repercussions. Krishna, the Supreme Authority and ultimate judge, explicitly warns in the Bhagavad Gita (16.23) about the fate of those who ignore divine guidance:

yaḥ śāstra-vidhim utsṛjya
vartate kāma-kārataḥ
na sa siddhim avāpnoti
na sukhaṁ na parāṁ gatim

'He who discards scriptural injunctions and acts according to his own whims attains neither perfection, nor happiness, nor the supreme destination.'

The Irony of Selective Faith

Yet, in today's world, many dismiss scriptures as outdated, irrelevant or impractical. Instead, they place blind faith in modern science, social media and popular opinion—without verifying the credibility of these sources. Theories change, news is often sensationalized and opinions shift with trends. Ironically, while scriptures that have stood the test of time are questioned, unverified claims from the Internet are readily accepted as truth.

This selective scepticism is concerning. In the name of 'practicality', people choose what is convenient, ignoring eternal truths. However, whether one acknowledges them or not, universal laws remain unchanged. The scriptures are not just religious texts; they are the instruction manuals for life, guiding humanity on how to live in harmony with natural and spiritual laws.

The Proof of Authenticity

For those who are sceptical, dismissing scriptures without proper investigation is unscientific. Even in science, a hypothesis is tested before being accepted or rejected. Similarly, one must evaluate the scriptures systematically. There are three key ways to test their authenticity:

1. Scriptures as Life Manuals

Whenever we purchase a gadget, it comes with a manual that explains how to operate it correctly. If we follow the instructions, the device functions optimally; if we disregard them, we risk damaging it. Similarly, the scriptures serve as the manual for human life.

Rather than rejecting them outright, why not apply their teachings and observe the results? Ancient wisdom such as meditation, yoga and kirtan—originating from these texts—are now globally embraced for their physical, mental and spiritual benefits. Those who follow scriptural principles experience peace and clarity, while those who ignore them often face turmoil.

2. Axiomatic Truths—Wisdom Ahead of Its Time

An axiomatic truth is self-evident, requiring no external validation. The Vedic scriptures contain many such truths, which were initially ridiculed but later confirmed by modern science. For instance:

- Cow dung is pure: Science now confirms that cow dung has antiseptic and medicinal properties.

- The Earth is round: This was asserted in the Vedas long before it was accepted by Western science.
- Plants have life: This fact, proven by scientist Jagdish Chandra Bose in the twentieth century, was already detailed in Vedic texts.
- Foetal development: The Shrimad Bhagavatam describes the growth of a foetus in the womb with astonishing accuracy—centuries before the advent of ultrasound technology.

If the scriptures were mere human creations, how could they contain knowledge that science would only later 'discover'?

3. Astonishing Predictions of the Future

Vedic scriptures have accurately predicted the appearance of great personalities and major societal shifts. Some examples include:

- Lord Buddha (Shrimad Bhagavatam 1.3.24)
- Chanakya and Chandragupta Maurya (Shrimad Bhagavatam 12.1.11–12)
- Sri Chaitanya Mahaprabhu (Mahabharata, Anushasana Parva 149.92), Shrimad Bhagavatam 11.5.32)
- Jesus and Prophet Muhammad (Bhavishya Purana, Atharva Veda Kanda 20, Shukta 127, 1–3)

The scriptures also contain chillingly accurate descriptions of societal decay in Kaliyuga (the present age):

- Food will be sold in markets: Once given freely as charity, food is now a commodity.
- People will eat the flesh of their own offspring: While shocking, reports of foetal consumption exist today.
- Power will define righteousness: Wealth and brute strength now command more respect than wisdom or virtue.
- Men will be judged by appearance, not character: The trend of equating long hair or fashion choices with beauty was foretold.

How could these predictions, written thousands of years ago, so precisely describe our modern world? The only logical conclusion is that these scriptures originate from a source beyond human intelligence.

Science vs Scriptures—A Changing vs Constant Truth

Scientific theories are in a constant state of flux. What was once accepted as fact is later disproven or revised. Even fundamental scientific concepts, such as Hubble's Constant (which defines the expansion rate of the universe), have changed so frequently that scientists now jokingly call it 'Hubble's Variable'.

In contrast, scriptural truths remain unchanged. The Bhagavad Gita, Shrimad Bhagavatam and Vedas have provided consistent wisdom for thousands of years, never needing revision. This itself is proof of their divine origin.

The Conclusion—Trust the Eternal Wisdom

Disregarding scriptural injunctions in favour of personal whims is like discarding a road map while traveling through an unfamiliar territory. While we may feel independent, the consequences of our actions will eventually manifest, just as defying physical laws (like gravity) results in injury.

The scriptures are not meant to restrict us but to elevate us. They provide a framework for living a fulfilling and meaningful life. By applying their principles, we align ourselves with the highest wisdom and experience true happiness.

Rather than dismissing them as outdated, let us take a moment to explore and test them. If they hold true—which they always have—then following them is not just a choice, but the most intelligent decision we can make.

41

Charity

Charity is not just a noble act; it is the sacred duty of every householder. It softens the heart, breaks the shackles of material attachment and helps us cultivate a spirit of conscious detachment. The more we cling to our possessions, the deeper we get trapped in the whirlpool of material existence. But when we give, we purify our wealth, our hearts and our consciousness.

Never Say No

If someone approaches us for help, we should never refuse. Every opportunity to share what we have is not a burden but a **blessing.** It is as if the universe is giving us a chance to be of use to someone in need. Instead of thinking, 'Why is this person asking me?' we should feel grateful and say, 'I have been chosen to help. I have been given the ability to give!'

However, charity is not just about giving away money or resources. It is a sacred act that must be performed with the right mindset and under the right conditions. Many people give, but without knowing the proper way to do it. In the Bhagavad Gita (17.20-22), Krishna explains that charity can be classified into three categories:

The Three Types of Charity

1. Charity in the Mode of Goodness (Sattvic Daan)

dātavyam iti yad dānaṁ
dīyate 'nupakāriṇe
deśe kāle ca pātre ca
tad dānaṁ sāttvikaṁ smṛtam

Bhagavad Gita (17.20)

'Charity given out of duty, without expectation of return, at the proper time and place and to a worthy person is considered to be in the mode of goodness.'

- Given with a pure heart
- No expectations of recognition or reward
- Done at the right time, place and to a worthy recipient

💡 **Example:** Helping someone who genuinely needs it, without expecting anything in return. Supporting a good cause selflessly.

2. Charity in the Mode of Passion (Rajasik Daan)

yat tu pratyupakārārthaṁ
phalam uddiśya vā punaḥ
dīyate ca parikliṣṭaṁ
tad dānaṁ rājasaṁ smṛtam

Bhagavad Gita (17.21)

'But charity performed with the expectation of some return, with a desire for fruitive results or in a grudging mood is said to be charity in the mode of passion.'

- Given with the expectation of getting something in return
- Done to gain name, fame or social status
- Given with reluctance or calculation

💡 **Example:** Donating to a cause only to get tax benefits or public recognition. Giving money to a beggar while thinking, 'I hope he thanks me!'

3. Charity in the Mode of Ignorance (Tamasik Daan)

adeśa-kāle yad dānam
apātrebhyaś ca dīyate

asat-kṛtam avajñātaṁ
tat tāmasam udāhṛtam

Bhagavad Gita (17.22)

'And charity performed at an impure place, at an improper time, to unworthy persons, or without proper attention and respect is said to be in the mode of ignorance.'

- Given without thought or care
- Donating to an unworthy cause
- Done in a way that humiliates the recipient

Example: Giving money to an addict who will use it for drugs. Throwing food at the poor instead of respectfully handing it to them.

How to Give Charity the Right Way

Simply giving away money is not charity. **Real charity must be done with awareness, respect and purity.** Here are a few principles to keep in mind when giving:

1. Give With a Sense of Duty, Not Compulsion

Charity should not feel forced. It should come from a place of gratitude and compassion. When we give out of duty, we do not feel superior to the one receiving—it becomes a sacred exchange.

2. Give to the Right Person, at the Right Time and in the Right Way

Helping someone in need is different from encouraging bad habits. **Be mindful of whom you are giving to and how your charity will be used.**

3. Give Wholeheartedly—It Should Pinch a Little

If charity does not challenge our attachment to wealth, it is not real charity. A billionaire donating a few thousand rupees is not a sacrifice. The true spirit of giving lies in parting with something valuable, not just excess.

Myth: Giving will make me poor.

Truth: The Vedas explain that charity is the gateway to wealth. What we give away comes back multiplied—maybe not from the same source, but from somewhere else.

The Golden Rule: Never Brag About Charity

The highest form of charity is done silently. The moment we announce our good deeds, we lose the spiritual benefit of the act. True generosity needs no audience.

Krishna Himself says in the Bhagavad Gita (3.13) that those who eat without first offering to others eat only sin. Our Vedic heritage is full of examples of kings and saints who gave without hesitation:

King Rantidev: A great king who was willing to sacrifice his own life to feed the starving guests who kept coming.

King Shibi: Offered his own flesh to save a helpless pigeon.

This is the standard we should aspire to.

Charity Should Fulfil the Need, Not the Ego

A common mistake people make when giving charity is doing it **the way they want, rather than how it is needed.**

Example:

- Someone needs school fees, but we give them food instead.
- A person asks for help with medical expenses, but we donate to an unrelated charity instead.

If our giving is centred around our preferences rather than the actual need, it is not true charity—it is just another form of self-satisfaction.

Real giving means being sensitive to what the other person truly requires, even if it is inconvenient for us.

The Takeaway

1. Charity purifies wealth and expands our consciousness.
2. Give with a pure heart, at the right time, place and to the right person.
3. The best charity is given selflessly, without expectation of return.
4. Give in a way that fulfils the real need, not just your personal preference.
5. Never publicize or brag about your charity—let it remain sacred.

The law of karma is simple: What we give, we receive. If we give generously, life will reward us abundantly. But more than material rewards, the real treasure lies in a purified heart—one that sees beyond selfish interests and acts as a true instrument of love and service.

The next time an opportunity to give comes your way, don't hesitate. It's not a loss—it's an invitation to rise higher.

42

Bhakti

Soul's Eternal Resting Place

Many people faint as soon as they hear the word 'bhakti'. What if we were told that it is the greatest power within the creation that conquers even the unconquerable? What if we were told that Krishna, the Supreme Being, actually longs to be conquered—not by strength, knowledge or wealth, but by love? What if the key to having a personal relationship with Him isn't found in complex rituals, intellectual debates or material success, but in something as simple as love and devotion?

Conquered by Love

In our world, we often measure power by how much control we have—over our careers, relationships and even our emotions. But Krishna, the all-powerful Supreme Lord, reveals something completely different. Despite being the master of all universes, He allows Himself to be bound, not by force, but by love. This is the essence of bhakti—devotion so pure and heartfelt that even Krishna cannot resist it.

The Gopis of Vrindavan had no education, and they were not high society girls of a city or a town. They were simple village girls. But they were such great devotees that Krishna was fully under their control and would dance to their tunes. They could chastise Krishna, bind Him and make Him dance in exchange for some buttermilk—and Krishna had to obey. This is the power of bhakti.

It is the only path that attracts Krishna as He Himself declares in the Bhagavad Gita (18.55):

bhaktyā mām abhijānāti
yāvān yaś cāsmi tattvataḥ
tato māṁ tattvato jñātvā
viśate tad-anantaram

'One can understand Me as I am, as the Supreme Lord, only by devotional service (bhakti). And when one is in full consciousness of Me by such devotion, he can enter into the Kingdom of God.'

The Only Auspicious Path

It is not just another spiritual path but the ultimate shortcut to connecting with Krishna, the most powerful, attractive yet loving personality in existence. It is the art of knowing and loving God and the only process that can pacify the eternal hankering of the soul. Neither karma, nor dhyana, jnana or yoga has any power to attract Krishna's attention. In all these, a person is more dependent on his or her own abilities to achieve spiritual perfection whereas in bhakti, a person simply surrenders and serves the Lord's will in divine love.

Why Do We Struggle to Connect?

Too many distractions, ignorance, lack of faith, misconceptions and our 'we know better' attitude stemming out of deep-rooted arrogance. In today's fast-paced world, we have access to limitless information. Everything is just a Google search away. We put faith in science, social media and self-help books but often feel disconnected from something deeper. Why? Because logic and material success alone cannot satisfy the soul, which is spiritual in nature and longs for a deeper spiritual connection with its source, Krishna. We all are parts and parcels of Krishna. We have an eternal relationship with Him, but we have forgotten. Bhakti is the most powerful way to reestablish that connection. Some know it and some do not, but Krishna Himself declares this truth in the Bhagavad Gita (15.7):

mamaivāṁśo jīva-loke
jīva-bhūtaḥ sanātanaḥ

manaḥ-ṣaṣṭhānīndriyāṇi
prakṛti-sthāni karṣati

'The living entities in this conditioned world are My eternal fragmental parts. Due to conditioned life, they are struggling very hard with the six senses, which include the mind.'

Krishna cannot be understood purely by the intellect. He is beyond scientific equations and philosophical debates. Just as we cannot analyse love with a microscope, Krishna must be experienced through the heart. Bhakti is not about external achievements—it's about creating an internal transformation that awakens divine love.

Though in the Bhagavad Gita, Krishna talks about various methods to connect with Him (karma, jnana and yoga), we see these discussed only in very few verses or one chapter for each. But for Bhakti Yoga, there are six full chapters (7–12). And other chapters also end with major emphasis on Bhakti Yoga.

What Is Bhakti? (And What It's NOT!)

Many misunderstand bhakti as mere ritualistic worship or blind faith. Some think it means renouncing everything and living in the mountains. Others assume it's an emotional crutch for those who cannot handle life's struggles. All of these are misconceptions.

Bhakti is the eternal occupation of the soul. It is love in action. It is not just devotion but **devotional service.** It is a deep, personal connection with Krishna that makes life more meaningful, joyful and fulfilling. Unlike mechanical religious practices, bhakti is dynamic—it can be expressed through music, art, service and even our daily responsibilities. If the goal of whatever we do is to please Krishna, it is bhakti. As simple as that.

In the Bhagavad Gita (9.22), Krishna assures us:

ananyāś cintayanto māṁ
ye janāḥ paryupāsate
teṣāṁ nityābhiyuktānāṁ
yoga-kṣemaṁ vahāmy aham

'To those who are constantly devoted and worship Me with love, I give the understanding by which they can come to Me.'

Bhakti is for everyone—not just monks or saints. Whether you are a student, an entrepreneur or a creative artist, bhakti can be seamlessly integrated into your life.

Bhakti Is Freedom, Not Restriction

One of the biggest misconceptions about bhakti is that it restricts life. People fear that surrendering to Krishna means giving up their independence. But real freedom is not doing whatever we want—it's being free from anxiety, stress and the emptiness of material pursuits.

- Bhakti is not about rules; it's about relationships.
- Bhakti is not about suppression; it's about expression—expressing love for Krishna in creative and personal ways.
- Bhakti is not about renouncing happiness; it's about discovering a deeper, lasting happiness.

Material success, relationships and entertainment can bring temporary pleasure, but only bhakti brings permanent joy as it directly addresses the needs of the soul, the real self.

The Power of Bhakti: The Shortcut to Krishna's Heart

Spiritual seekers struggle for lifetimes, climbing mountains of austerity, drowning in oceans of knowledge—while a simple devotee crosses the distance in a single leap, powered by bhakti.

Bhakti is the only path where the devotee becomes greater than God Himself. Not that he wants to be greater than Him, but subdued by a devotee's love, Krishna puts Himself under the control of His devotee. If bhakti is a fire, then Krishna is like butter—He cannot resist melting in its warmth.

A poor woman in Vrindavan offered Krishna a handful of fruits with pure love. In return, Krishna filled her basket with precious jewels.

Krishna's childhood friend Sudama, a poor Brahmana, offered Him simple broken rice with love. Krishna, moved by his devotion, transformed his life with unlimited riches.

When Draupadi was being humiliated in the Kaurava court and no one came forward to help her, she surrendered to Krishna with complete faith, and instantly, Krishna became her protector.

These episodes show that Krishna is not interested in wealth, intellect or status—He only responds to bhakti.

What Is in It for Me?

Most people feel inspired only when there is some benefit in an activity. When it comes to bhakti, the art of serving Bhagwan, we might doubt, 'Why do I need to do it? How will it help me?'

1. **Divine grace:** In life, not everything is dependent on our efforts. When things are beyond our control, we will need grace to uplift us and open closed doors. Bhakti will fetch us that divine grace.
2. **Supreme protection:** Krishna personally stands with a devotee, protecting him from all dangers. Even though the Kauravas were greater in number and

had more powerful warriors on their side, they lost, and the Pandavas came out of the war unharmed because Krishna protected them throughout.

3. **Removes lamentation, confusion and fear/worry:** Shrimad Bhagavatam beautifully discusses the power of bhakti in (1.7.7);

   yasyāṁ vai śrūyamāṇāyāṁ
   kṛṣṇe parama-pūruṣe
   bhaktir utpadyate puṁsaḥ
   Śoka-moha-bhayāpahā

   'Simply by giving aural reception to this Vedic literature, the feeling for loving devotional service to Lord Krishna, the Supreme Lord, sprouts up at once to extinguish the fire of lamentation, illusion and fearfulness.'

Anyone who faithfully engages in bhakti by listening to the Shrimad Bhagavatam will have all the negativity countered.

4. **Freedom from sinful reactions:** Bhakti removes sinful karmas and thus the root cause of distress. One of the characteristics of bhakti is '*kleshagni*': it burns our anxiety to ashes. Any number of problems in our lives, even a small amount of distress or setback, is due to our sinful karmas committed in the past, knowingly or unknowingly.

The practice of bhakti neutralizes sinful karmas, thus ushering in a new life of good fortune for the devotee.

5. **Desires:** We have countless desires. The present day 'manifestation' techniques won't be of much help. If everything was possible simply by visualizing that something has already been accomplished or by writing at 3:33 a.m. every morning, then what about destiny? Why is everyone still not successful? Destiny is much bigger than us. If something is not in our destiny, no matter how many mundane techniques we apply, we will not be successful. But there is one factor bigger than destiny: the will or grace of the Supreme Lord. He can turn things around and change even our destiny. If He is pleased with us, and bhakti is the only way to please Him, then we will get more than what we desire and deserve. Little Dhruva was given a kingdom greater than his great-grandfather Lord Brahma. The only reason: because the Lord was pleased with his devotional service. Desires get fulfilled only by Krishna's grace. There is no other way. Therefore, the path of bhakti is supremely beneficial.

How to Practice Bhakti in Daily Life

It is a life of connection, not rejection. We don't need to leave our job, shave our head or move to a temple to practice bhakti. Here are five most potent ways (as mentioned by the great Vaishnava Acharya Shri Rupa Goswami) to perform bhakti in our everyday life. Even if a person is a neophyte on the path or a beginner, even a little connection with any of these five practices will bring him to an exalted spiritual status very, very quickly. We should practice at least one of these, if not more, to experience a wonderful transformation. But most important: these must be performed under the guidance of the devotees of the Lord. The five most powerful forms of Bhakri are:

1. Studying the Shrimad Bhagavatam: a sacred text describing the Lord's beautiful pastimes.
2. Chanting His holy names: Krishna's names cleanse the heart and fill us with joy. Try chanting *Hare Krishna, Hare Krishna, Krishna Krishna, Hare Hare/Hare Rama, Hare Rama, Rama Rama, Hare Hare* and see the difference.
3. Worshipping the deity of the Lord: offering aarti, food, flowers, incense, Tulsi, jewellery and other relevant items.
4. Residing in a holy place: Just by residing in a holy place such as Vrindavan (even if for a short while) or a temple of the Lord, our devotional sentiments awaken, and we get inspired to engage in bhakti practices. In addition, any devotional act performed in a holy place yields spiritual benefits a million times more than any other place.

5. Serving the Vaishnavas or devotees of the Lord: Devotees are dearer to Krishna than His own life. When we serve devotees, we make quick spiritual advancement by His grace.

In addition, we can include the following practices as per our time and capacity:

1. Listening to kirtan: Instead of endless Netflix or random playlists, try listening to devotional music. The energy of kirtan transforms the atmosphere instantly.
2. Offering our food: Before eating, offer your food to Krishna with love. This simple act purifies what we consume and elevates our consciousness.
3. Serving others: Whether it's feeding someone, helping a friend or volunteering, acts of kindness done seeing others as His loving children connect us to Him.
4. Letting go and surrendering: Instead of stressing over everything, learn to trust Krishna. This doesn't mean being passive but understanding that Krishna has a perfect plan. Having faith in God means having faith in His timing.

Krishna is not far away. For a devotee, He is available 24x7. He is closer than we think—waiting for us to take the first step. He is waiting to help us, provided we turn to Him. The beauty of bhakti is that it doesn't require qualifications. We don't need to be perfect, pure, or even religious. We just need to begin.

We may not have anything to offer—no wealth, no intelligence, no beauty—but if we offer our heart with sincerity, Krishna will be ours forever.

Kings rule empires, warriors win battles, scholars master knowledge—but the one who possesses bhakti rules over Krishna Himself.

So, the real question is: Are we ready to take the first step?

43

Surrender

If we want to understand the real message of any book, where should we look? The end.

That's where the author leaves the final, most important takeaway.

The Bhagavad Gita is no different. After teaching Arjuna about duty, self-control, devotion, knowledge and different paths to success, Krishna closes with one ultimate instruction—forget everything else and do just one thing.

He says in Bhagavad Gita (18.66):

sarva-dharmān parityajya
mām ekaṁ śaraṇaṁ vraja
ahaṁ tvāṁ sarva-pāpebhyo
mokṣayiṣyāmi mā śucaḥ

> 'Abandon all varieties of religion and just surrender unto Me. I shall deliver you from all sinful reactions. Do not fear.'

Think about that. After all the knowledge Krishna shared, His **final message** isn't about rituals, philosophies, or moral codes. It's **simple:**

> **'Trust Me. Surrender to Me. And I'll take care of everything.'**

True Meaning of Surrender

The word surrender may sound scary, but only because we lack a proper understanding of what it truly implies. It's the most beautiful experience, but only those who have done it will ever understand.

A child is carefree and fearless because he is fully surrendered to his parents and thus, all his needs are automatically taken care of. Two enemy soldiers are fighting against each other with bullets being shot from both sides. However, as soon as one of them surrenders to the other, the bullets stop. It is a crude example but enough to drive home the point.

Surrendering to God (Krishna) stops the onslaught of miseries we go through in life. Suppose a criminal has been sentenced to ten years in prison for his disobedience to the laws of the government. But as soon as he surrenders to the will of the government and begins to behave nicely, his sentence may be reduced, or he may be freed immediately as per the order of the supreme authority of the state. Similarly, we remain under the laws of Karma as long as we live a life independent of God. As soon as we surrender, our miseries begin to end.

The Shelter That Never Fails

A beautiful example of it is found in the Ramayana in how Vibhishana, the younger brother of the mighty demon Ravana, comes to surrender to Lord Ram, seeking His shelter.

When the monkeys in Lord Ram's army see him coming, many of them get alarmed and start picking up their weapons. Lord Ram asks some of the senior members of the army whether Vibhishana should be accepted. Some say he could be a spy, so better to avoid contact with him. Some suggest killing him immediately because, after all, he is the brother of Ravana, the cruellest personality of the time, and thus cannot be trusted. Some remain confused.

Only Hanumanji speaks in favour as he has been witness to Vibhishana's devotional attitude towards Lord Ram at the time of his visit to Lanka in search of Mother Sita. After consulting with them all, Lord Rama reveals His compassionate heart and says, 'I was just testing you all. What to speak of Vibhishana, even if Ravana comes now and surrenders, he shall also be forgiven.'

Then, the Lord recites the following verse, which is considered to be the conclusive message of the Ramayana:

> *sakrudeva prapannaya tavasmiti cha yachate*
> *abhayam sarva bhutebhyo dadami etat vratam mama*
>
> 'If a person even once surrenders and takes shelter in me saying, "My dear Lord, from this moment I am yours", from that moment I take complete charge of that person's life and grant him eternal fearlessness by protecting from all others. This is my vow.'

The Essential Message of all Scriptures

Whether we talk about the Bhagavad Gita, the Ramayana, the Shrimad Bhagavatam or any other scripture, the essential message remains the same:

1. Anything can happen at any moment. There is a danger at every step, and
2. If we take shelter in the Lord or seek His help by chanting His names, remembering Him or praying to Him, all dangers can be averted.

Life is uncertain, but divine shelter is not. The world may shake beneath our feet, but those who hold on to the Lord remain unshaken. Just like a child instinctively runs to the parent in fear, we too are invited to run to Krishna—for protection, peace and inner strength.

How to Surrender?

Now, the next question could be: I do not know whether I can surrender. Well, we have all done it at some point in our life. Whenever we go through any issues in life, have we not sought the help of others? Haven't we ever surrendered to our own intelligence? Have we not taken shelter of various processes to resolve our issues? All of these are instances of surrendering. Surrender, in more sublime words, is taking shelter with someone for help, and doing what the person wants us to do. And how does Krishna want us to surrender, or what does He want us to do? He has explained in Bhagavad Gita (18.65):

> *man-manā bhava mad-bhakto*
> *mad-yājī māṁ namaskuru*
> *mām evaiṣyasi satyaṁ te*
> *pratijāne priyo 'si me*

> 'Always think of Me, become My devotee, worship Me and offer your homage unto Me. Thus, you will come to Me without fail. I promise you this because you are my very dear friend.'

Essentially, surrendering to Krishna means becoming His devotee by following the process He has given.

If we engage in the devotional service of Krishna as mentioned above, He promises to take complete charge of our life. The easiest way and the greatest expression of our surrender in today's day and age is chanting of His holy names:

> *Hare Krishna, Hare Krishna, Krishna Krishna, Hare Hare/Hare Rama, Hare Rama, Rama Rama, Hare Hare*

> Lord Brahma tells Narada Muni in the Kali-santarana Upanishad:

> *iti ṣoḍaśakaṁ nāmnāṁ*
> *kali-kalmaṣa-nāśanam*
> *nātaḥ paratаropāyaḥ*
> *sarva-vedeṣu dṛśyate*

> 'After searching through all the Vedic literature, one cannot find a method of religion (dharma) more sublime for this age than the chanting of the sixteen syllable Hare Krishna maha-mantra.'

In the Mundaka Upanishad it is stated:

> *dvāparīyair janair viṣṇuḥ*
> *pañcarātrais tu kevalaiḥ*
> *kalau tu nāma-mātreṇa*
> *pūjyate bhagavān hariḥ*

'In the Dvapar Yuga, people should worship Lord Hari only by the regulative principles of the deity worship. In the Age of Kaliyuga, however, people should simply chant the holy names of the Supreme Lord.'

Krishna Enters, Karma Exits

No matter what we do in life, our ultimate goal is to be happy. What stops us from being happy? Problems. What is the root cause of all our problems? Our past karmas. Thus, as soon as we surrender to, or take shelter with Krishna, as promised by Him, He forgives and dissolves our karmas. When the root cause of all our miseries is gone, how will we ever experience any problems in life?

So, next time you are in trouble, do not get anxious or start running around. Sit in one place, bring the form of Krishna in your mind and start chanting His names . . .

Hare Krishna, Hare Krishna, Krishna Krishna, Hare Hare/Hare Rama, Hare Rama, Rama Rama, Hare Hare

. . . and you will witness all the closed doors opening, and everything in life falling into place.

44

The Greatest Service (Seva)

People worship God (Krishna) in so many ways. Some offer elaborate rituals, others cook delicious food for Him and many spend their time maintaining grand temples, intricately carved and beautifully decorated.

These are all wonderful ways to express devotion. But have you ever stopped to ask:

What does God want the most?

A Father's Constant Anxiety

Imagine a wealthy father—he has palatial homes, endless riches, influence and the finest food at his table. But there's one problem—his children have rebelled and left him.

No matter how much luxury surrounds him, can he truly enjoy any of it? Absolutely not. His mind and heart will always be longing for his children to return.

Now, think about God. He owns everything. The entire universe—every planet, every ocean, every star—is already His. There's nothing we can give Him that He doesn't already have.

Except for one thing: Our love.

When we turn away from Him, we become like lost children—caught up in the distractions of the world, forgetting our real home. But just like the loving father, Krishna's greatest desire isn't our offerings—it's us.

If an ordinary father in this world thinks like this, then Krishna, our Supreme Father, whose affection for us is far greater than millions of fathers combined, certainly feels the pain of His children, who have turned away from Him.

He Is Constantly Trying

He wants us to be back with Him. He is constantly making plans for our return to Him because it's not just about His happiness in our reunion with Him. He knows that we will only be happy when we are reconnected with Him. He has this great anxiety—and anyone who helps Krishna relieve Himself of this anxiety by taking up the task of connecting others to Him becomes most dear to Him. As He Himself says in the Bhagavad Gita (18.69):

na ca tasmān manuṣyeṣu
kaścin me priya-kṛttamaḥ
bhavitā na ca me tasmād
anyaḥ priya-taro bhuvi

> 'There is no servant in this world dearer to Me than he, nor will there ever be one more dear.'

Thus, the greatest, most confidential service we can ever render to Krishna in order to be immediately recognised by Him is to utilize our God given intelligence to connect others to the path of Krishna consciousness, thus making their lives auspicious.

How to Connect?

The first and most important thing in spiritual life isn't expertise, talent or knowledge—it's sincerity.

Krishna doesn't expect us to be scholars or saints overnight. He simply looks at our desire. If we truly want to serve Him, He will empower us in ways we never imagined. So, how can we share Krishna's message with the world? There's something for everyone.

1. Share What You Know

If you have a gift for speaking, talk about Krishna. Share what you've learned from the Bhagavad Gita and Vedic literature. We don't need to be experts. Just pass on what you've heard from devotees.

And here's the amazing part—when Krishna sees our sincere effort, He will reveal deeper truths to you from within your heart. The more you share, the more you'll become a channel for His wisdom.

2. Invite Others to Spiritual Gatherings

Maybe you feel like you don't know enough to teach—that's okay! Just invite people to events where expert and sincere devotees are speaking. Let them hear Krishna's message directly.

A simple invitation can change someone's life.

3. Distribute Spiritual Books

Not everyone is ready for a deep conversation about spirituality, but almost everyone is curious.

Giving someone a spiritual book (like the Bhagavad Gita) plants a seed. Even if they don't read it immediately, Krishna will awaken their interest at the right time.

4. Share Prasad—Transform Lives

Prasad (food offered to Krishna) isn't ordinary food—it's packed with spiritual potency. When someone eats prasad, it gradually transforms their mind and heart, dissolving negative karma and bringing them closer to Krishna.

It's a simple but powerful way to help others—without saying a single word.

5. Support Those Who Are Actively Preaching the Message

If you can't do any of the above, you can support those who are already doing it.

1. Help organize events.
2. Volunteer your time and skills.
3. Donate to spiritual projects.
4. Offer resources to help spread Krishna's message.

Everything—whether it's money, effort or even just encouragement—counts as service to Krishna.

Krishna Uses Whatever We Offer

The beautiful thing about Bhakti (devotion) is that Krishna accepts whatever we can sincerely offer—whether it's our words, our time, our resources, or even just a desire to serve.

The key is to start somewhere. Once we take a step forward, Krishna guides us further.

So, what can we do today to share Krishna's message? Even the smallest effort can change someone's life—and make our own life spiritually successful.

Do Something

People are suffering—even if they don't realize it. We do. And if we know the truth, it's on us to wake them up. The root cause of all suffering? Forgetting Krishna.

We need to remind them, reach them, and use every means necessary to bring them back to the forgotten path. Because that's what life is for—service. But what kind of service?

- **Body-level Service:** Food, shelter and medicine.
- **Soul-level Service:** Helping people reconnect with God.

Most of the world is stuck on just helping the body. But we're not the body. We are eternal souls residing in temporary shells.

No matter how much we try to fix the body, it will perish. The real person is the soul, and true help means caring for both—with priority on the soul.

Why? Because Karma Is Real

The real reason people suffer? Karma. And no medicine, no charity, no therapy can erase karma. That's like saving the coat of a drowning man but letting him sink.

As long as karma remains, suffering continues—it just takes different forms. The only way out? Serving Krishna. When people surrender to Him, they break free from the cycle of karma and suffering—for good.

Want to Truly Help? Bring People to Krishna

The highest act of compassion isn't just feeding mouths—it's feeding souls. If you really care, don't stop at temporary relief. Guide people toward eternal freedom.

And here's the best part: Krishna sees it all. If we help others find Him, He helps us—He showers His mercy, and our life becomes truly successful.

So, are we ready to make a real difference and become most dear to Him?

45

Krishna, the All Auspicious

Is Krishna Really the Cause of Conflict? Or the Cure for It?

In many homes today, people hesitate to keep a copy of the Mahabharata. Why? Because of a popular superstition: 'If we keep Mahabharata at home, there will be a Mahabharata (war) in our house too.' Some even avoid placing the Bhagavad Gita or a painting of Krishna and Arjuna on the chariot, fearing it might invite quarrels or unrest.

Let's pause for a moment and ask a simple question: Do families without the Gita or Mahabharata at home live completely peaceful lives, free from arguments and problems?

Clearly not.

So, where did this idea come from? It's not from the scriptures. It's not from the saints. It's from centuries of subtle misinformation designed to disconnect people from their roots and their greatest source of strength—**Krishna.**

If remembering Krishna or keeping His image causes problems, then why does the last verse of the Bhagavad Gita(18.78) say this?

> *yatra yogeśvaraḥ kṛṣṇo*
> *yatra pārtho dhanur-dharaḥ*
> *tatra śrīr vijayo bhūtir*
> *dhruvā nītir matir mama*

> 'Wherever there is Krishna, the master of all mystics, and wherever there is Arjuna, the supreme archer, there will also certainly be opulence, victory, extraordinary power, and righteousness. That is My opinion.'

That doesn't sound like a warning—it sounds like a divine guarantee. In fact, Krishna doesn't bring conflict—He brings clarity. He doesn't ignite quarrels—He ends them. He doesn't bring bad luck—He burns bad karma.

Have we not heard the age-old saying, '*A family that prays together, stays together*'? It is the presence of Krishna that unites, uplifts and purifies.

The Vedas and Puranas repeatedly affirm that anything connected to the Lord is inherently auspicious. As the Ramcharitmanas beautifully states:

'Mangal bhavan, amangal haari'—'The Lord is the abode of all auspiciousness, and the remover of all inauspiciousness.'

And the Purana verse says:

> *oṃ apavitraḥ pavitro vā sarvāvasthāṃ gato'pi vā*
> *yaḥ smaret puṇḍarīkākṣaṃ sa bāhyābhyantaraḥ śuciḥ*
>
> 'Whether pure or impure, in any condition whatsoever, one who remembers Krishna becomes pure inside and out.'

Krishna's name, form, books, and deity are undifferentiated from Him. When we bring any of these into our lives, we are not decorating our homes—we are transforming them into sacred spaces.

Think about it:

- A regular meal becomes prasad when offered to Krishna.
- A regular building becomes a temple when He is worshipped there.

- Even a jail in Mathura has become a pilgrimage site—not because of its architecture, but because Krishna was born there.

So let's ask again—how can someone who purifies everything He touches ever bring misfortune?

Even when Krishna appeared to punish demons, He was actually giving them liberation. That's the kind of 'harm' He does—He harms our ignorance, our ego, and our suffering. And even that is a blessing in disguise.

Once Krishna enters your life, nothing remains ordinary. Your home becomes a temple. Your heart becomes a sanctuary. Your karma becomes a testimony to His grace.

So don't fear the Gita. Don't fear the Mahabharata.

And most importantly, don't fear Krishna. Fear forgetting Him.

Because *anything that reminds us of Him can only bring good fortune, never misfortune.*

Let us not shut the door to our best friend based on baseless fear. Instead, let us open our hearts and homes to Him—through His holy name, His form, His words and His devotees—and watch how life transforms, not with conflict, but with peace, power and purpose.